Characterizing and Exploring the Implications of

MARITIME IRREGULAR WARFARE

MOLLY DUNIGAN | DICK HOFFMANN
PETER CHALK | BRIAN NICHIPORUK | PAUL DELUCA

Prepared for the United States Navy

NATIONAL DEFENSE RESEARCH INSTITUTE

The research described in this report was prepared for the United States Navy. The research was conducted within the RAND National Defense Research Institute, a federally funded research and development center sponsored by the Office of the Secretary of Defense, the Joint Staff, the Unified Combatant Commands, the Navy, the Marine Corps, the defense agencies, and the defense Intelligence Community under Contract W74V8H-06-C-0002.

Library of Congress Cataloging-in-Publication Data

Characterizing and exploring the implications of maritime irregular warfare / Molly Dunigan ... [et al.].
    p. cm.
  Includes bibliographical references.
  ISBN 978-0-8330-5891-1 (pbk. : alk. paper)
  1. Naval art and science. 2. Irregular warfare—United States—Case studies.
  3. Riverine operations—United States—Case studies. 4. Piracy—Prevention—Case studies. 5. Maritime terrorism—Prevention—Case studies. I. Dunigan, Molly.

    V103.C44 2012
    359.4'2—dc23

                                                                              2012002819

The RAND Corporation is a nonprofit institution that helps improve policy and decisionmaking through research and analysis. RAND's publications do not necessarily reflect the opinions of its research clients and sponsors.

RAND® is a registered trademark.

Cover photos: (top) U.S. Navy photo; (bottom) Crown Copyright/UK Ministry of Defence, used in accordance with the Open Government License.

Published 2012 by the RAND Corporation
1776 Main Street, P.O. Box 2138, Santa Monica, CA 90407-2138
1200 South Hayes Street, Arlington, VA 22202-5050
4570 Fifth Avenue, Suite 600, Pittsburgh, PA 15213-2665
RAND URL: http://www.rand.org/
To order RAND documents or to obtain additional information, contact
Distribution Services: Telephone: (310) 451-7002;
Fax: (310) 451-6915; Email: order@rand.org

Preface

In light of ongoing U.S. involvement in the conflicts in Iraq and Afghanistan, the concept of *irregular warfare* has become prevalent in U.S. defense strategy and doctrine. Irregular warfare (IW) includes a variety of land-, air-, and maritime-based activities, yet current conceptions of irregular warfare do not focus on the specific requirements and opportunities related to conducting IW in the maritime realm. Although ground forces carry out the bulk of irregular warfare activities, maritime-based forces also play an important role in IW campaigns. The purpose of this analysis is to describe the strategic potential of maritime irregular warfare (MIW) and to assess its operational and tactical characteristics based on a sample of recent MIW operations. The results are intended to inform future U.S. investments in force structure and future IW doctrine regarding the ways in which MIW fits with other IW domains.

This monograph should be of interest to policymakers, military personnel, and others interested in the intersection of irregular warfare and maritime force. Readers may also find the following RAND publications to be of interest:

- *The Maritime Dimension of International Security: Terrorism, Piracy, and Challenges for the United States*, by Peter Chalk, MG-697-AF, 2008
- *Building Partner Capacity to Combat Weapons of Mass Destruction*, by Jennifer D. P. Moroney and Joe Hogler, with Benjamin Bahney, Kim Cragin, David R. Howell, Charlotte Lynch, and S. Rebecca Zimmerman, MG-783-DTRA, 2009

- *Ungoverned Territories: Understanding and Reducing Terrorism Risks*, by Angel Rabasa, Steven Boraz, Peter Chalk, Kim Cragin, Theodore W. Karasik, Jennifer D. P. Moroney, Kevin A. O'Brien, and John E. Peters, MG-561-AF, 2007
- *Small Ships in Theater Security Cooperation*, by Robert W. Button, Irv Blickstein, Laurence Smallman, David Newton, Michele A. Poole, and Michael Nixon, MG-698-NAVY, 2008.

This research was sponsored by the U.S. Navy Special Warfare Command and conducted within the International Security and Defense Policy Center of the RAND National Defense Research Institute, a federally funded research and development center sponsored by the Office of the Secretary of Defense, the Joint Staff, the Unified Combatant Commands, the Navy, the Marine Corps, the defense agencies, and the defense Intelligence Community.

For more information on the International Security and Defense Policy Center, see http://www.rand.org/nsrd/ndri/centers/isdp.html or contact the director (contact information is provided on web page).

Contents

Figures and Table

Figures

Table

Summary

Given U.S. involvement in and support for multiple counterinsurgency (COIN) and counterterrorism (CT) campaigns in various theaters, particularly over the past decade, the concept of *irregular warfare* has become increasingly prevalent among defense strategists and analysts (HQDA, 1961, 2006, 2008; U.S. Joint Chiefs of Staff, 2008; Newton et al., 2009). Irregular warfare (IW) includes many more activities than just COIN and CT, and, despite the fact that some of these campaigns are occurring or have occurred in maritime environments, current conceptions of irregular warfare do not focus on the specific requirements and opportunities related to conducting IW in the maritime realm (Mullins, undated).[1]

While we recognize that ground forces carry out the bulk of irregular warfare activities, the purpose of this analysis is to describe the strategic potential of maritime irregular warfare (MIW) and to assess its operational and tactical characteristics based on a sample of recent MIW operations. In doing so, we aim to inform future U.S. investments in force structure and future IW doctrine regarding the maritime aspects of IW and how they fit with other IW domains. Although maritime forces are often employed primarily in support of ground operations, our research shows that—in environments with a maritime component—maritime operations tend to have a noticeable comparative advantage over land-based operations in terms of mobility and can involve a smaller or less visible footprint in a host nation. Thus,

---

[1] This is true even of the Navy Irregular Warfare Office's definition of the term.

the conceptions of IW, which do not currently include a prominent maritime component, could benefit from increased recognition of the unique contributions that maritime operations could make to overall IW campaigns.

The potential for maritime operations to play a role in IW campaigns raises the question of which maritime operational activities might be most relevant in the IW context and, furthermore, what implications such operations might have for the overall strategic environment and force structure. Guided by these questions, this monograph defines MIW in relation to IW doctrine and identifies the actors and tactics involved in a range of cases. It also provides a detailed analysis of a sample of historical and current MIW activities from both a friendly and enemy viewpoint.

What Is Maritime Irregular Warfare?

Based on our doctrinal and case-study analyses, we define MIW as operations involving at least one irregular actor or tactic that aim to shape the maritime environment in at least one of three ways: (1) to prevent supplies or personnel support from reaching an adversary, (2) to increase the capacity of partner naval and maritime forces, or (3) to project tailored U.S. power ashore to directly confront adversary forces, when necessary.

Building on this definition, we also identify three types of operational activities conducted in MIW, as shown in Figure S.1: external operations, building partner capacity, and internal operations.

Finally, we identify a spectrum of strategic scenarios in which MIW tends to occur. This spectrum ranges from law enforcement scenarios, such as counterpiracy (CP) or counternarcotics (CN) campaigns, to unconventional warfare (UW) and COIN.

Figure S.1
The Range of MIW Operational Activities

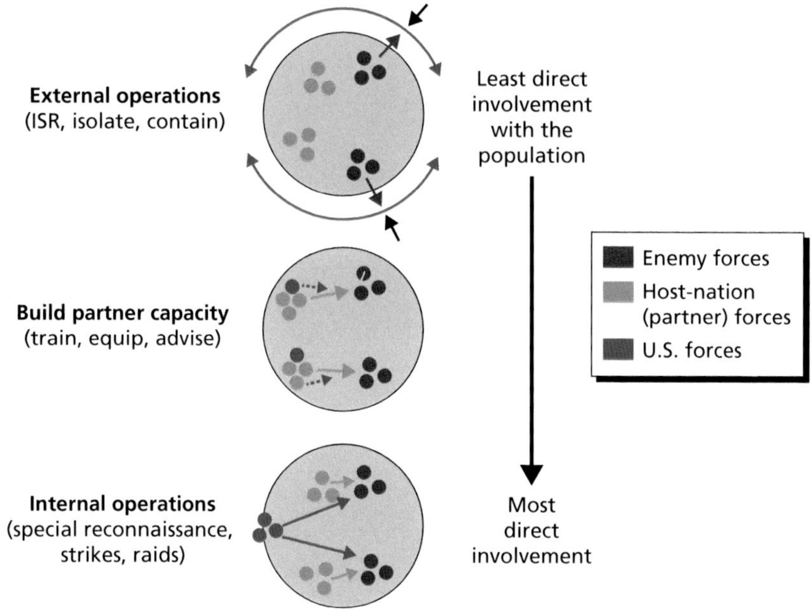

External operations
(ISR, isolate, contain)

Least direct
involvement
with the
population

Build partner capacity
(train, equip, advise)

■ Enemy forces
■ Host-nation
   (partner) forces
■ U.S. forces

Internal operations
(special reconnaissance,
strikes, raids)

Most
direct
involvement

NOTE: ISR = intelligence, surveillance, and reconnaissance.
RAND MG1127-S.1

Maritime Irregular Warfare Case Studies

Operation Enduring Freedom–Philippines (OEF-P), in which the U.S. force has been limited to 600 personnel in the joint operations area, served as a benchmark case of MIW in our study for several reasons. Of primary importance for this analysis, the operation is being conducted in an archipelago environment, in which we would expect maritime forces to play a large role, and includes, to some extent, irregular forces and tactics on both sides of the conflict. Moreover, the enemy in this case (Abu Sayyaf) utilizes maritime methods to a significant extent. Thus, the operation appears on the surface to be a model case of maritime irregular warfare. Finally, the operation is largely considered a successful case of irregular COIN and CT warfare conducted by U.S. forces. Upon closer examination, the OEF-P case reflects the strategic, operational, and tactical challenges of MIW as well as its potential benefits.

This study compared and contrasted the OEF-P case with several historical cases of MIW spanning the range of strategic scenarios in which MIW tends to occur in an effort to determine the extent to which the lessons of OEF-P are generalizable. Other historical cases examined included MIW operations during the Vietnam War (an example of COIN), ongoing MIW CN/CT operations in Colombia and counterpiracy operations off the Horn of Africa (HoA) (both examples of law enforcement-related operations), and the covert U.S. mining of Nicaraguan ports and harbors in the early 1980s (an example of UW).[2]

The study also examined several cases illustrating the breadth of capabilities possessed by adversaries or analogous actors in the recent past and in current operations. While the future is uncertain regarding the range of potential MIW threats that the United States may confront, we found this exercise useful in clarifying the spectrum of possible future irregular threats that the United States may confront in the maritime environment. The Colombia case provides some insight into the issue of potential future threats, as do the cases of the Sea Tigers (the maritime wing of the Liberation Tigers of Tamil Eelam, or LTTE) active in Sri Lanka from 1984 through 2009, the Lashkar-e-Taiba (LeT) attack on Mumbai in 2008, and piracy in the HoA over the past decade. While the LTTE, LeT, and HoA pirates are not all direct adversaries of the United States at present, they can inform future U.S. approaches to MIW threats. Taken together, these cases paint a picture

---

[2]   While the lessons of the Nicaragua case are useful, one should exercise caution in generalizing from this case study to other cases of maritime unconventional warfare. This case is unique in that the U.S. partner (the Contras) was aware of the mining operations only after the fact, and CIA-hired contractors—rather than U.S. military or partner forces—conducted the operations assessed here. We nonetheless consider this a case of unconventional warfare due to the fact that the United States was engaged in a broader UW mission to support the Contras during this period, and the maritime operations were a component of a broader strategy aimed specifically at establishing conditions for the partner forces to succeed. Other cases of UW operations in the maritime realm might lead to different findings, however. Analyses of such cases would therefore pose a fruitful avenue for future research.

of current and potential future MIW adversaries who possess a vast range in technical capability but are often well organized, employ successful recruitment tactics, and are quite adept at intelligence, surveillance, and reconnaissance.

Findings and Recommendations

U.S. and Partner Capabilities

The study's main findings span the strategic, operational, and tactical levels. Several are specific to MIW, while others have implications both for MIW and for IW operations more broadly.

First, *the maritime force is generally considered to play a supportive role to ground forces in IW and therefore has the potential to be underutilized even in IW operations conducted in a predominantly maritime environment.* Because much IW takes place on land and is conducted by ground forces, maritime forces often play a largely supportive role in land-based IW operations. This is true even in maritime environments, such as the Philippine archipelago. Therefore, policymakers and military planners should weigh the costs and benefits of land-based versus maritime operations in each IW situation and make balanced assessments regarding the extent to which each option provides a viable solution on its own and in combination with other options. It is also relevant to note, from a tactical planning perspective, that maritime forces sometimes conduct IW operations in nontraditional environments (such as on land) and perform nontraditional functions (such as leading provincial reconstruction teams and building schools). This has occurred in Colombia, Operation Iraqi Freedom, and Operation Enduring Freedom in Afghanistan. Conversely, ground-based forces sometimes conduct maritime operations in IW campaigns, as was seen in Vietnam. Moreover, the Vietnam case illustrates that riverine MIW can benefit from a combined-arms approach, so it is sensible to consider how maritime and ground-based forces can be used in tandem to conduct MIW operations.

Second, *countries that have a prevalent maritime dimension associated with an insurgency could potentially benefit from the enhancement of civil-military operations (CMOs) in the maritime arena.* The Vietnam experience shows that in riverine COIN—just as in land-based COIN—strike operations against the main insurgent units should be followed up by efforts to enhance local public support if final victory is to be achieved; CMOs provide one potential mechanism for enhancing public support. Such operations might, for instance, aim to revitalize ports and harbors in areas that are largely economically dependent on fishing. They have also been conducted to some extent in OEF-P, but land-based efforts have thus far been the focus of CMOs in that largely maritime environment.

Third, *maritime operations in IW can allow the United States to scale its ground involvement in useful ways.* Because MIW capabilities often allow U.S. forces to operate with relatively high mobility, low visibility, and a small footprint, maritime forces offer a military option when host-nation sensitivities or U.S. preferences constrain the deployment of U.S. ground forces. For example, sea-based forces in the Sulu Archipelago are more mobile, responsive, and capable of supporting Armed Forces of the Philippines (AFP) missions across larger coastal areas of the archipelago than are land-based special forces teams.

Fourth, if one assumes that future MIW engagements that entail building a partner's capacity will resemble OEF-P, *it is important to manage strategic expectations based on realistic assessments of the partner's capabilities.* By properly scaling U.S. efforts in a way that ensured that the AFP remained in the lead while also ensuring its success, the IW campaign in OEF-P has encouraged development and promoted the AFP's legitimacy among the Filipino population. The personnel limits and other constraints placed on U.S. forces in OEF-P are argued to be one reason that the Philippines is investing more in its navy and developing practical new capabilities for the Sulu Archipelago, such as the Coast Watch South coastal surveillance system paired with additional combatant craft. Yet, scaling U.S. activities and strategic expectations in this manner can be challenging, particularly when U.S. forces must limit their own activities and sacrifice short-term effectiveness for long-term partner viability.

Fifth, *when building partner capacity, either in MIW or land-based IW, the United States should make efforts to provide equipment and tech-*

nology that the partner will be able to maintain and operate without difficulty. This lesson is particularly evident in the OEF-P case. Because of the Philippines' minimal military-industrial infrastructure and its navy's small training budgets, U.S. forces need to pass along equipment and teach tactics that are low-tech, low-cost, practical, reliable, and easy to maintain. Another equipment-related problem in the context of building partner capacity has been evident in the United States' gifting of old or obsolete equipment to the Philippine Navy, which creates problems in accessing spare parts. In many cases, the Philippine Navy has managed to build its own spare parts, but it is worthwhile to note that this is a potential challenge facing partnering nations that have unequal technical capabilities and types of equipment (author interviews with Philippine Navy personnel, January 2009).

Sixth, *with regard to operational methods, coastal maritime interdiction can play an instrumental role in setting the conditions for success in IW by cutting the supply lines that sustain an insurgency.* Previous research on COIN has shown that the presence or absence of sanctuary for the insurgents is a very important variable determining the success of the COIN force (Gompert and Gordon, 2008). As such, maritime approaches can become an important domain of irregular warfare as insurgents work to keep open and exploit sea lines of communication and counterinsurgents seek to disrupt these lines and use them to support their own mobility and logistics. This was demonstrated in various maritime operations in the Vietnam War and has been successfully employed in Colombia as well. Coastal and riverine interdiction may also be easier to conduct than ground interdiction when enough intelligence, surveillance, and reconnaissance assets and naval platforms are devoted to the task on a constant basis.

Seventh, as the Nicaragua case illustrates, *U.S. partners in MIW may only have to influence and monitor the sensibilities of a local population, but the legitimacy of U.S. involvement may be tested in worldwide public opinion.* Revelations of U.S. involvement in the mining of Nicaraguan harbors earned the United States international condemnation, with the Sandinistas introducing a resolution in the United Nations Security Council denouncing the United States for "the escalation of acts of military aggression brought against" Nicaragua and Nicaragua asking the International Court of Justice to find the mining and U.S. support of the Contras a violation of international law. The stakes for the United States—as a global power—may therefore be higher, and it may have more to lose than do its partners, even though U.S. partners may face most of the operational dangers. While the Nicaragua case is so unique that it may not be generalizable to other cases of UW in maritime environments, this particular lesson applies to any MIW activities in which the United States or other global powers engage.

Finally, *international cooperation in confronting MIW adversaries is often necessary, and the U.S. Navy should make an effort to ensure that it is tactically and operationally interoperable with partner navies in order to facilitate coordination.* This is illustrated by the case of counterpiracy off the HoA, but it is more widely applicable due to the international nature of the maritime environment.

Adversary Capabilities

Several findings relate specifically to adversary capabilities. For one, it is important to note that *an adaptive and technically proficient irregular enemy can challenge maritime forces in irregular warfare.* This can be seen in the Colombian narco-traffickers' switch from moving large shipments of cocaine in single consignments on fishing trawlers to using go-fast boats to smuggle smaller amounts in stages, a change that was initiated following several major drug seizures between 2002 and 2006. The traffickers' heightened use of semi- and fully submersible vessels to smuggle drugs out of the country is another example; this practice has increased with the growth of U.S. and Colombian naval capabilities to catch traffickers' go-fast boats.

The case of the LeT attacks in Mumbai illustrates the advantages that could accrue to a terrorist enemy from a maritime approach to a target. A maritime approach can allow operatives to avoid border crossings and airport security, can offer opportunities to quietly hijack a local vessel so that attackers can blend in with the normal local coastal traffic, and can offer terrorist teams some extra time for preattack planning as well as extra time for rest just before the attack commences. Finally, a maritime insertion can allow terrorists to select very precise landing sites and infiltration routes.

The case of the LeT attacks in Mumbai also illustrates the disadvantages that can accrue to a terrorist enemy from a maritime approach to a target. First, once a full blown, large-scale urban assault has started, it can be very difficult to exfiltrate the operatives. Second, the transport of large explosives aboard crude fishing vessels and trawlers is risky; thus, maritime terrorist strikes might be limited to relying on small arms to do their damage. Third, some kind of reconnaissance cell would likely have to be sent to the target city well in advance of the attack, creating opportunities for a skilled intelligence service to place surveillance teams on the reconnaissance cell and break up the plot before the assault team can embark. Moreover, a maritime approach does not allow the terrorist team to fully disperse until it lands ashore. Even if the operatives approach in two or three different small boats, the interception of just one of the boats could drastically reduce the team's numbers and effectiveness.

Finally, it is instructive to note that *despite relatively low technological prowess, pirate gangs in the HoA have exhibited an ability to act extremely far out to sea and have displayed both good surveillance and reconnaissance practices and a system of tacit knowledge regarding the characteristics of vessels that are susceptible to attack.* The case of piracy off the HoA also illustrates that future MIW adversaries may pose a threat that is more economic than strategic or military. Furthermore, these financial costs might be imposed with relatively minimal investments backing the operations themselves.

Recommendations

The findings presented here have several direct implications for the U.S. conventional Navy and Naval Special Warfare Command (NSW). First, U.S. naval forces should continue to provide U.S. partners with suitable equipment that they will be able to operate and maintain and should continually strive to increase their interoperability with partner forces. Second, U.S. naval forces may have to continue or expand training of partner forces to confront future MIW threats. Third, when conducting MIW, operating from a sea base offers advantages to NSW. However, due to the costs of such a practice, both NSW and the conventional Navy must also recognize that decisions regarding when and where to support sea basing of this sort need to be made carefully. Fourth, in support of future MIW operations, NSW is likely to have ongoing requirements for maritime interdiction and containment. Fifth, the United States could benefit from maintaining operational and tactical capabilities with which to assist its partners in surveillance, particularly against small submarines and mining threats. Sixth, NSW should consider increasing its capacity to conduct maritime-based CMOs.

Conventional U.S. naval forces should similarly consider their role in supporting significant irregular ground operations launched from the sea, as well as their role in interdiction and containment campaigns. In contrast to those of NSW, conventional U.S. Navy capabilities to support IW might entail CMOs and related activities to a greater extent than direct action.

In addition to these recommendations specific to NSW and conventional naval forces, this monograph makes several broader policy-relevant recommendations pertaining to MIW. First, to prevent and deter against maritime attack approaches such as that seen in the Mumbai case, policymakers around the globe might consider funding and maintaining large, high-quality coast guards. Second, to counter the threat of piracy, the international community might consider placing automated hijack alert systems on larger fishing vessels and trawlers (comparable to panic buttons in U.S. banks), which would allow the crews of large and medium-sized fishing vessels to quickly broadcast encrypted hijack distress signals to regional navies and coast guards. Third, to prevent and deter MIW attacks more broadly, intelligence agencies should consider increasing their surveillance of maritime training programs at jihadist camps in Pakistan, Yemen, and (especially) Somalia. These agencies should also work to prevent pirates and jihadists from joining forces in the HoA. Finally, it would be sensible to fund expanded measures to prevent jihadists from embarking on attack operations from certain high-threat ports, such as Karachi, Aden, and Mogadishu.

Acknowledgments

Many people supported and contributed to this research. CAPT Rick Sisk and Jim Stokes from U.S. Naval Special Warfare Command, sponsored this study and provided professional and decisive guidance. We also thank the many anonymous operators, staff officers, military planners, and civilian officials who generously gave their time to provide insights, observations, and recollections of their experiences with policies, plans, and operations in the southern Philippines. We also benefited from the patience and assistance with our requests for information from personnel from U.S. Pacific Command; U.S. Special Operations Command, Pacific; Joint Special Operations Task Force–Philippines; Joint U.S. Military Assistance Group–Philippines; the U.S. Agency for International Development; Naval Special Warfare Group 4; and Naval Special Warfare Group 1. We received outstanding support from officers in the Australian Defence Force, the Australian Department of Foreign Affairs and Trade, the Australian Agency for International Development, the Government of the Republic of the Philippines, and the Armed Forces of the Philippines.

This monograph benefits from the insights we received from colleagues at the Naval Postgraduate School, and we are indebted to Keenan Yoho for his hospitality and assistance in organizing this exchange of ideas. We owe great thanks to RADM Raymond C. Smith, U.S. Navy (retired); RADM Cathal L. "Irish" Flynn, U.S. Navy (retired); and Adam Grissom and Gordon Lee at RAND for their input and feedback. Moreover, we are very appreciative of the support and guidance we received from the International Security and

Defense Policy Center in the RAND National Defense Research Institute, particularly from Michael Lostumbo and James Dobbins. Finally, we are grateful to Stephanie Lonsinger for her extensive assistance in formatting the manuscript and to editor Lauren Skrabala, production editor Jocelyn Lofstrom, and artist Mary Wrazen for their work in producing the final monograph.

The resulting document, of course, remains the sole responsibility of the authors.

Abbreviations

AFP	Armed Forces of the Philippines
ARMM	Autonomous Region in Muslim Mindanao
ASG	Abu Sayyaf Group
BPC	building partner capacity
CIA	U.S. Central Intelligence Agency
CMO	civil-military operation
CN	counternarcotics
COIN	counterinsurgency
CP	counterpiracy
CT	counterterrorism
CTF	combined task force
DoD	U.S. Department of Defense
ELN	Ejército de Liberación Nacional [National Liberation Army]
EUNAVFOR	European Union Naval Force
FARC	Fuerzas Armadas Revolucionarias de Colombia [Revolutionary Armed Forces of Colombia]
FATA	Federally Administered Tribal Areas

FM	field manual
FDN	Fuerza Democrática Nicaragüense [Nicaraguan Democratic Force]
FID	foreign internal defense
GPS	Global Positioning System
GRP	Government of the Republic of the Philippines
HoA	Horn of Africa
ISR	intelligence, surveillance, and reconnaissance
IW	irregular warfare
JOC	Joint Operating Concept
JP	joint publication
JSOTF-P	Joint Special Operations Task Force–Philippines
JTF	joint task force
LeT	Lashkar-e-Taiba
LPD	U.S. Navy designation for an amphibious assault ship
LST	landing ship, tank
LTTE	Liberation Tigers of Tamil Eelam
MACV	U.S. Military Assistance Command, Vietnam
MCO	major combat operation
MILF	Moro Islamic Liberation Front
MIW	maritime irregular warfare
Mk V SOC	Mark V Special Operations Craft
MNLF	Moro National Liberation Front

MOOTW	military operations other than war
MRF	Mobile Riverine Force
NATO	North Atlantic Treaty Organization
NSW	U.S. Navy Special Warfare Command
OEF	Operation Enduring Freedom
OEF-P	Operation Enduring Freedom–Philippines
OIF	Operation Iraqi Freedom
PSYOP	psychological operations
QDR	Quadrennial Defense Review
RIB	rigid-hull inflatable boat
RPG	rocket-propelled grenade
SHADE	Combined Maritime Forces Shared Awareness and Deconfliction
SPSS	self-propelled semi-submersible
SSTR	stability, security, transition, and reconstruction
SWCC	U.S. Navy Special Warfare Combatant-Craft Crewman
T-AK	U.S. Navy designation for a maritime pre-positioning force cargo ship
UNSCR	UN Security Council Resolution
USAID	U.S. Agency for International Development
UW	unconventional warfare
VC	Viet Cong

CHAPTER ONE

Introduction

Given U.S. involvement and support for multiple counterinsurgency (COIN) and counterterrorism (CT) campaigns in various theaters, particularly over the past decade, the concept of *irregular warfare* has become increasingly prevalent among defense strategists and analysts, with numerous policy publications and field manuals devoted to defining, explaining, and exploring the consequences of the term and related activities (HQDA, 1961, 2006, 2008; U.S. Joint Chiefs of Staff, 2008; Newton et al., 2009). Indeed, CT expert William Rosenau (2006, p. 53) notes that "insurgency and counterinsurgency . . . have enjoyed a level of military, academic, and journalistic notice unseen since the 1960s." Irregular warfare (IW) includes many more activities than just COIN and CT and, despite the fact that some of these campaigns are occurring or have occurred in maritime environments, current conceptions of IW do not focus on the specific requirements and opportunities related to conducting such operations in the maritime realm. This is true even of the U.S. Navy Irregular Warfare Office's definition of the term, which includes the following activities in its notion of IW: counterinsurgency (COIN); unconventional warfare (UW); counterterrorism (CT); foreign internal defense (FID); stability, security, transition, and reconstruction (SSTR) operations; strategic communication; psychological operations (PSYOP); information operations; civil-military operations (CMOs); intelligence and counterintelligence activities; transnational criminal activities that support or sustain IW, such as narco-trafficking, illicit arms dealing, and illegal financial transactions; and law-enforcement activities focused on countering irregular adversaries (Mullins, undated). Several of these activities have an analogous maritime component, but IW focused specifically on maritime capabilities has been largely absent from discussions regarding irregular warfare up to this point.

While we recognize that ground forces often carry out the bulk of IW activities, the purpose of this analysis is to describe the strategic potential of maritime irregular warfare (MIW) and to assess its operational and tactical characteristics based on a sample of recent MIW operations. In doing so, we aim to inform future U.S. investments in force structure and future IW doctrine regarding the maritime aspects of IW and how they fit with other IW domains. Although maritime forces are often employed primarily in support of ground operations, our research shows that—in environments with a maritime component—maritime operations tend to have a noticeable comparative advantage over land-based operations in terms of mobility, freedom of maneuver, and the ability to impose a smaller or less visible footprint on a host nation. Thus, current conceptions of IW, which do not include a prominent maritime component, could benefit from increased recognition of the unique contributions that maritime operations could make to overall IW campaigns.

This potential for maritime operations to play a role in IW campaigns raises the question of which maritime operational activities might be most relevant in the IW context and, furthermore, what implications such operations might have for overall strategic and force structure considerations. With an eye to answering these questions, this monograph defines MIW based on IW doctrine and the actors and tactics involved in numerous cases of IW. It also provides a detailed analysis of the range of historical and current MIW activities from both a friendly and enemy viewpoint.

Methodological Approach

We used comparative case studies to explore the range of possible MIW activities in which the United States, its allies, and its enemies could engage.[1] We first conducted an in-depth examination of the case of Operation Enduring Freedom–Philippines (OEF-P) as a benchmark case of irregular operations in an archipelago environment, then compared and contrasted this operation with a range of other MIW cases selected to show variance across actors, tactics, and strategic context. To be included in the analysis, at least one party to the conflict had to employ irregular forces, the tactics used had to—at least in part—be irregular, and the operations had to be conducted in a maritime environment; the sample included riverine operations, operations at sea, and operations in close proximity to the shore.

Organization of This Monograph

Chapter Two examines the literature on IW and develops a working definition of, and framework of analysis for, MIW. Chapter Three looks in depth at the study's benchmark case of IW conducted in a largely maritime environment (OEF-P) to glean an understanding of the tactical, operational, and strategic concerns related to the use of maritime forces to pursue IW objectives in a largely maritime environment. Chapter Four then assesses several historical and modern case studies of MIW operations in COIN, UW, and law-enforcement scenarios, such as CN, CT, and counterpiracy (CP), deriving additional lessons for MIW beyond those provided by the OEF-P case. Chapter Five explores three recent cases in which MIW capabilities were effectively utilized by adversary forces, demonstrating the potential range of threats that the United States may face in this realm in the future. The monograph concludes with lessons regarding MIW's strategic potential and operational and tactical considerations for the future.

---

[1] The study's dependent variable was conflict processes and outcomes in maritime warfare environments, and the independent variable was IW operations in an environment with a significant maritime component. We selected our cases for variance on the independent variable because, as King, Keohane, and Verba (1994, p. 140) note, "the best 'intentional' design selects observations to ensure variation in the explanatory variable (and any control variables) without regard to the values of the dependent variables."

CHAPTER TWO

What Is Maritime Irregular Warfare?

Irregular warfare is a term used by the U.S. Department of Defense (DoD) to describe certain military operations. The 2006 Quadrennial Defense Review (QDR) introduced the term in the context of one of four types of threats facing the United States (irregular threats; the other three were traditional, disruptive, and catastrophic) and suggested that more U.S. DoD plans and funding should be devoted to IW programs (DoD, 2006).[1] Yet, there is still debate in DoD doctrine and among military and policymaking circles regarding the exact definition of IW. Perhaps in recognition of this lack of clarity, the term *irregular warfare* is used only once in the 2010 *Quadrennial Defense Review Report*, even though many of the activities frequently considered to constitute IW are still discussed at length in that document (DoD, 2010a).

In examining the meaning of MIW in this chapter, we first consider IW more generally. Because these are DoD terms, we do not presume to define them for DoD; rather, we review DoD doctrine, publications, and reports concerning IW to ascertain a theoretical and doctrinal definition of IW. However, U.S. literature on IW does not devote much attention to the issue of maritime operations. Therefore, to develop an understanding of MIW, we review past military operations considered to be cases of IW that were conducted in maritime environ-

---

[1] The 2006 QDR (p. 3) defines IW as "conflicts in which enemy combatants are not regular military forces of nation-states." However, as discussed later in this monograph, numerous other factors are often considered when determining whether a conflict qualifies as irregular warfare.

ments. The MIW concept developed through this chapter's doctrinal and case-study analysis serves as the definition of MIW throughout the remainder of this monograph.

Doctrinal Conceptions of Irregular Warfare

The Joint Warfighting Center published a literature review in 2006 that examined the ambiguities related to irregular warfare (Joint Warfighting Center, 2006). The review rejects the term as too vague and ill defined. An article aptly titled "Irregular Warfare: Everything Yet Nothing" (Stevenson et al., 2008) echoes this point and typifies numerous articles and essays in defense journals. Moreover, two annual reports to Congress on Navy IW in 2009 and 2010 described the confusion regarding the definition of IW and the Navy's broad list of IW activities (O'Rourke, 2009, 2010).

The common complaint in the literature is that IW is too broad a concept to be useful. It includes special operations, combat operations, and humanitarian activities; indeed, the only point of agreement seems to be that IW does not include decisive combat operations during a major combat operation (MCO)—for example, during the invasion of Iraq in March 2003. With that understanding, DoD officials have been reluctant to narrow the broad array of non–MCOs with a more useful definition of IW and, more importantly, to identify and exclude those non-IW activities that may not rouse much budgetary attention. All of these factors lead to confusion surrounding the definition of IW.

To sift through this confusion, we start with the most commonly accepted definition and deduce IW's fundamental principles and components. The Secretary of Defense–approved definition of IW laid out in Joint Publication (JP) 1-02 and reiterated in both the September 2007 and May 2010 versions of the IW Joint Operating Concept (IW JOC) is as follows:

> A violent struggle among state and non-state actors for legitimacy and influence over the relevant populations. Irregular warfare (IW) favors indirect approaches, though it may employ the

full range of military and other capabilities, in order to erode an adversary's power, influence, and will. (DoD, 2007, 2010b; see also U.S. Joint Chiefs of Staff, 2011b)

From this definition, we deduce that IW involves a population, an adversary, and indirect approaches. Furthermore, IW also involves U.S. forces in some role, and the reference to "indirect approaches" implies the existence of some sort of partner through which U.S. forces can act indirectly. The JP 1-02 definition also provides the caveat that IW may include direct operations as well. However, IW's main objectives are legitimacy and influence over the population, not necessarily the destruction or defeat of the adversary. Therefore, direct operations in IW should be undertaken only to influence how the population perceives the legitimacy of U.S. and partner forces.

The term's use stems in part from the COIN and stabilization operations in Operation Iraqi Freedom (OIF) and Operation Enduring Freedom (OEF). The literature on IW also includes references to the UW campaign during the earlier years of OEF in Afghanistan, when U.S. special forces partnered with the Northern Alliance. U.S. military doctrine explains these military operations as components of foreign internal defense (FID), which in its entirety includes all U.S. support for host-nation internal defense and development (even direct U.S. combat operations).[2]

It is fairly common practice to define IW in a way that encompasses COIN, FID, and UW. But the IW literature also includes CT, SSTR, law enforcement against transnational crime, CMOs, information operations, and other military activities less clearly related to IW as it is defined in JP 1-02 and both versions of the IW JOC. This broader list of military activities leads one to question whether IW essentially

---

[2] FID is a special operations core task in which U.S. forces train a legitimate partner, such as the Iraqi Security Forces or the Afghan National Army. UW is also a special operations core task in which U.S. forces train and organize a revolutionary partner striving to overthrow the existing government, such as the Northern Alliance in Afghanistan or the Contras in El Salvador. See Field Manual (FM) 3-24 on COIN (HQDA, 2006), FM 3-05 and JP 3-05 on UW and FID (HQDA, 2010; U.S. Joint Chiefs of Staff, 2011a), and the most recent IW JOC (DoD, 2010b).

constitutes all warfare activities short of decisive combat operations in an MCO. In fact, all-inclusive concepts of less-conventional military operations have been included in joint doctrine under the category of "military operations other than war" (MOOTW). The 2001 version of JP 3-0, *Joint Operations*, included several examples of MOOTW. For reference, the examples of MOOTW listed in the 2001 version of JP 3-0 were as follows:

- arms control
- combating terrorism
- consequence management
- DoD support to counterdrug operations
- domestic support operations
- enforcement of sanctions and maritime intercept operations
- enforcing exclusion zones
- ensuring freedom of navigation and overflight
- foreign humanitarian assistance
- noncombatant evacuation operations
- peace operations
- protection of shipping
- recovery operations
- show-of-force operations
- strikes and raids
- support to COIN
- support to insurgency (U.S. Joint Chiefs of Staff, 2001, p. V-6).

However, DoD thinking has since evolved, and the 2008 version of JP 3-0 abandoned the notion of MOOTW in favor of three categories of military operations: (1) major operations and campaigns, (2) crisis response and limited contingency operations, and (3) military engagement, security cooperation, and deterrence.

The 2007 IW JOC began to narrow down the list of activities considered to be IW. Figure 2.1, drawn from the 2007 IW JOC, shows the distinctions between IW, stabilization operations, and major combat operations (DoD, 2007). The 2010 version of the IW JOC goes further, identifying five main IW activities: CT, UW, FID, COIN, and

Figure 2.1
Irregular Warfare, Major Combat Operations, and Stabilization, Security,
Transition, and Reconstruction Joint Operating Concepts

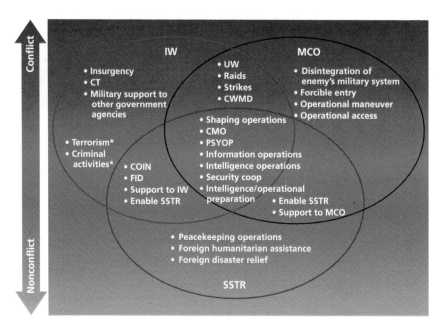

SOURCE: DoD, 2007, p. 15, Figure 3.
NOTE: * Indicates adversary concept. CWMD = counter–weapons of mass destruction.
RAND MG1127-2.1

stability operations. It also, however, recognizes several key activities related to IW, including strategic communication, information operations of all kinds, PSYOP, CMOs, and support to law enforcement (DoD, 2010b). In doing so, it risks broadening the concept once again to the point where it is no longer analytically useful.

From this review of existing IW doctrine, it is clear that IW generally involves U.S. forces working with partners, against adversaries, in a violent struggle for legitimacy in which indirect operations are preferred over direct operations (although both may occur). This doctrinal conception of IW does not sufficiently describe maritime roles in such operations, however. Indeed, the Navy Irregular Warfare Office defines IW as follows:

IW emphasizes the use of indirect, non-conventional methods and means to subvert, attrite, and exhaust an adversary, or render irrelevant, rather than defeat him through direct conventional military confrontation. (Mullins, undated)

Notably, none of the various joint or Navy definitions of IW specifically mention maritime activities in either a positive or negative sense, indicating that IW strategy neither emphasizes nor rules out maritime operations. We therefore examine cases of IW in maritime environments in an effort to derive a more complete understanding of MIW.

Maritime Irregular Warfare in Practice

To contribute to filling the void of information on maritime activities in IW, we analyzed eight historical cases of IW operations that included a maritime component. In doing so, we sought to build knowledge about the actors and methods involved in MIW specifically, as opposed to IW more generally. These cases were selected based on two key defining criteria: each involves IW operations, as defined in JP 1-02, and each includes maritime activities or activities conducted in a maritime environment.

To select our cases, we assembled a broad list of contingencies—including maritime operations—that might be considered examples of IW. While this is certainly not an exhaustive list of potential cases, we aimed to develop a balanced pool of cases that varied in terms of actors and tactics. Table 2.1 presents these cases and is organized according to the types of friendly and enemy forces involved in each contingency.

From this comparison, we eliminated the cases in which conventional friendly forces operated against conventional enemy forces, deeming those cases to constitute the early stages of a potential MCO rather than irregular operations. In other words, both the threats and the responses to those threats were more direct than in the cases examined in the following chapters. We also determined that these cases of friendly conventional forces versus enemy conventional forces did not

Table 2.1
Cases of MIW Organized by the Actors Involved

	Enemy Conventional Forces	Enemy Irregular Forces
Friendly Conventional Forces	Cold War—ISR (SSN vs. *Typhoon*-class submarine) Cold War—ISR (P-3 Orion, CVBG vs. Soviet Surface Action Group, Bear-D) ISR vs. USSR, China, North Korea	**Vietnam—Operation Game Warden, Operation Coronado, Operation Sealords** Libya—Operation El Dorado Canyon Lebanon—USS *New Jersey* naval gunfire support **Sri Lanka vs. Sea Tigers** Solomon Islands—Regional Assistance Mission to Solomon Islands Israel vs. Hezbollah OEF HoA Tomahawk missile strikes in Somalia **Mumbai—LeT** **Colombia COIN/CT/CN operations** **CTF-150/151 HoA**
Friendly Irregular Forces	WWII—Navy Scouts and Raiders Bay of Pigs **Vietnam—Operation Market Time** Panama—Operation Just Cause **Nicaragua—mining of ports** Persian Gulf—Operation Earnest Will Iraq—Operation Desert Storm (Phases I and II) Iraq—OIF (Phases I and II)	**Vietnam—Operation Sealords** Persian Gulf—Operation Earnest Will **OEF-P** Israel vs. Hezbollah **Mumbai—LeT** Spain vs. So San (North Korean freighter)

NOTE: The cases chosen for the in-depth analysis described in Chapters Three, Four, and Five are highlighted in bold. CTF = combined task force. CVBG = U.S. Navy classification for aircraft carrier battle group. HoA = Horn of Africa.
ISR = intelligence, surveillance, and reconnaissance. LeT = Lashkar-e-Taiba.
SSN = U.S. Navy classification for fast-attack nuclear submarine.

involve partners per se; this is a key component of IW as defined in doctrine, so the lack of partners in these cases provided another reason to eliminate them from our analysis.

What remains is a list of cases involving friendly special forces against either conventional or irregular enemy forces and cases involving friendly conventional forces against irregular enemy forces. From this list, we chose eight cases with significant, relevant operations that spanned the possible spectrum of MIW:

1. The United States in Vietnam:
    a. U.S. maritime security operations in Operation Market Time off the coast of Vietnam, 1965–1973
    b. U.S. COIN operations in Operation Game Warden in the Vietnam Mekong Delta, 1965–1968
    c. U.S. kinetic operations in the Coronado campaign in the Vietnam Mekong Delta, 1967–1968
    d. U.S. COIN operations in Operation Sealords in the Vietnam Mekong Delta, 1968–1971
2. U.S. UW operations in Nicaragua, 1981
3. Liberation Tigers of Tamil Eelam (LTTE) Sea Tigers UW operations in Sri Lanka, 1984–2009
4. U.S. counternarcotics (CN) operations in Colombia, 1990–present
5. U.S. COIN and CT operations in support of the Armed Forces of the Philippines (AFP) in OEF-P, 2001–present
6. LeT attack in Mumbai, India, 2008
7. U.S. maritime security operations for CTF-150 off the HoA, 2002–present
8. U.S. counterpiracy (CP) operations for CTF-151 off the HoA, 2009–present.

We found that MIW comprises, at various times, both irregular and conventional warfare activities, perpetrated by both irregular and conventional forces, against irregular and conventional enemies. The combination of actors and methods involved determines whether the activity in question qualifies as MIW, in our view. To do so, at least one actor must be irregular (DoD, 2010b, pp. 9–10)[3] and the operations must take place in a maritime environment. We recognize that riverine operations are qualitatively distinct from maritime operations in that they are essentially an extension of land operations relying on rivers for mobility. However, we included them in our analysis because they entail the use of maritime capabilities and therefore may inform our understanding of MIW and MIW capabilities.

Because we sought to examine cases that included IW operations as defined in JP 1-02, many of these cases involved a state (such as the United States) providing some form of assistance to a partner (either a host-nation or nonstate force). This allowed us to include cases with indirect lines of operation on the part of the United States (or other intervening state). For example, in OEF-P, the United States has provided security force assistance to the Philippine military as it seeks to root out the terror threat posed by Abu Sayyaf in the post-9/11 environment (G. Wilson, 2006; Bakshian, 2007; Fridovich and Krawchuk, 2007).

Maritime Irregular Warfare Operational Activities: A Conceptual Framework

Based on our doctrinal and case-study analyses, we define MIW as operations involving at least one irregular actor or tactic that aim to shape the maritime environment in at least one of three ways: (1) to prevent supplies or personnel support from reaching an adver-

---

[3] This component of our definition is in line with the concept of IW laid out in the 2010 IW JOC, which states,

> For the purpose of this concept, irregular threats are those posed by a) non-state actors and b) state actors who adopt irregular methods. This concept recognizes that irregular methods may also be used against state actors who present more or less conventional threats, though this is not a focus of this JOC. (DoD, 2010b, pp. 9–10)

However, our definition goes beyond those in the 2010 IW JOC (DoD, 2010b) and the 2006 QDR (DoD, 2006) in its inclusion of conflicts in which friendly irregular forces confront enemy conventional forces, as well as its consideration of the nature of both the actors *and* tactics involved.

sary, (2) to increase the capacity of partner naval and maritime forces, or (3) to project tailored U.S. power ashore to directly confront adversary forces, when necessary.

In our review of MIW in practice, we see three broad types of operational activities used to shape the maritime environment: external operations, building partner capacity, and internal operations. Figure 2.2 shows these operational activities in order of their degree of involvement with the relevant population, from least to most direct.

External Operations

The first operational activity is external operations, in which U.S. or coalition forces operate in international waters, the territorial waters of a partner nation, international airspace, or a border nation. External operations aim to isolate the adversary within the population by preventing outside support or supplies from entering into the area of oper-

Figure 2.2
The Range of MIW Operational Activities

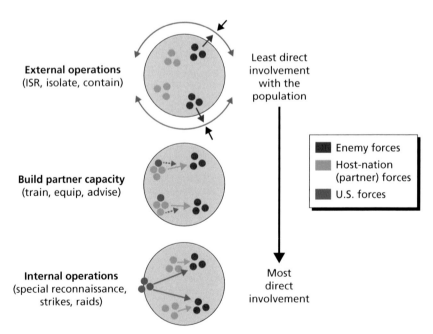

ations and to contain the adversary's influence by preventing it from spreading outside the area of operations. External MIW operations might include ISR missions, enforcement of exclusion zones through screening and maritime interdiction, or enforcement of no-fly zones. Because these operations do not occur directly among the population, they are not limited to any significant degree in terms of conventional capability, footprint, or firepower.

Building Partner Capacity

The second MIW operational activity is building partner capacity (BPC), in which U.S. or coalition forces train, equip, and advise a partner's forces so that they can defeat the adversary. This operational activity normally requires U.S. or coalition advisers to deploy to or near the area of operations and maneuver within the population as they train and advise the local forces. Therefore, these are relatively indirect efforts compared to internal operations, but they are more direct than external operations. Because BPC operations occur among or in close proximity to the population, they are limited by the extent to which the population is receptive to these forces' presence. Of note, BPC is often described by the phrase "train, advise, assist." We intentionally leave "assist" out of the BPC line of operation as presented here because we consider such operations to constitute the third type of MIW operational activity, internal operations.

Internal Operations

Internal operations are situations in which U.S. or coalition forces conduct either direct operations against an adversary among the population or indirect operations to assist a partner nation. Internal MIW operations include strikes, raids, or assaults designed to attrite the adversary and secure the population to a level at which the partner can begin operating successfully. Internal operations also include medical evacuation, quick-reaction force reinforcement, logistical support, maritime mobility insertion and extraction of partner forces, air mobility insertion and extraction of partner forces, special reconnaissance missions, and CMOs. In internal operations, U.S. and coalition forces conduct the most direct type of operations in the area of operations where the population and the adversary coexist. Consequently, these operations require the most discretion and sensitivity to the population's perception of who is legitimately responsible for security and governance. Indiscriminate, excessive force that causes extensive collateral damage and death is often counterproductive in these situations, as it can undermine the population's perception of U.S. and coalition legitimacy.

External, BPC, and internal operations can be considered components of MIW when they involve maritime forces or afloat forward operating bases or staging bases or when they occur in maritime environments. The three operational activities, along with our definition of MIW, serve as a conceptual framework for the remainder of this monograph, helping to organize our observations and findings with regard to the detailed case studies in Chapters Three through Five.

Spectrum of Strategic Scenarios Relevant to MIW

Through our examination of IW doctrine and our exploration of MIW in practice, we identified a spectrum of MIW that spans strategic scenarios—from law-enforcement scenarios, such as CP or CN campaigns, to UW and COIN campaigns. These strategic scenarios all include partners that could or should provide security, if conditions are set for their success, and U.S. or coalition forces that assist those partners' efforts against an adversary with external, BPC, or internal operations.

The conceptual framework encompassing these three strategic scenarios, in combination with the range of operational activities outlined in this chapter, works in the manner illustrated by the following example. In CTF-151's CP mission off the coast of Somalia, pirates threaten populations of merchant mariners. The coalition is conducting external operations to prevent the pirates from attacking the merchants (who are considered the coalition's partners in this case), as well as to limit resources to the pirate groups based ashore. Coalition forces assist the merchants with communication and provide advice, and, in the event that the pirates seize a vessel, they may conduct an internal operation to rescue the merchants. BPC is limited in this case, but there are efforts to train, equip, and advise merchant crews so that they can defend themselves, along with efforts to augment those crews with private shipboard security teams, which would also act as partners with CTF-151. Although the definition of MIW proposed earlier does not necessarily require all three operational activities to be present for a case to be considered MIW, this example of a law-enforcement operation does include all three.

Our definition of MIW also clarifies which activities do *not* constitute IW. For example, humanitarian assistance, disaster relief, CMOs, or noncombatant evacuations alone are not irregular warfare. These examples of MOOTW may be part of an IW campaign, but they do not necessarily include violent struggles, partners, or adversaries. CMOs in Iraq, Afghanistan, and the Philippines are important components of those respective COIN campaigns because they build infrastructure and partner legitimacy, but CMOs in Korea for a project that is unrelated to a broader IW campaign do not qualify as IW. Furthermore, U.S. operations designed to directly influence a conventional opponent, such as ISR near North Korea or freedom-of-navigation missions near China, are not considered IW or MIW. There is no lever for indirect operations (the crux of IW) in these examples, because neither example includes a partner or third-party population whose security is inherently threatened.

The MIW concept developed in this chapter contributes to an understanding of how maritime operations fit into IW doctrinally and in practice and how joint operations contribute to IW objectives in maritime environments. Utilizing the conceptual framework of MIW developed here, the next three chapters explore MIW case studies in an effort to devise recommendations regarding future strategic, operational, and tactical MIW capabilities.

The Case of Operation Enduring Freedom– Philippines

Concern in U.S. Pacific Command about terrorism and crime in the southern Philippines spiked a few months before September 11, 2001. On May 27 of that year, the Abu Sayyaf Group (ASG) kidnapped 17 Filipinos and three Americans from their diving resort cabins on Palawan Island. In this instance, ASG members covertly entered the resort by boat, captured their victims from seaside cabins, and then returned by boat to their camp on Basilan Island in the Sulu Archipelago—a classic amphibious raid (M. Bowden, 2007).[1]

After the September 11 attacks, the U.S. Pacific Command received orders to develop plans for defeating terrorist groups throughout the Pacific theater, including the ASG. U.S. Special Operations Command, Pacific, had already been coordinating contingency plans with the AFP through the Pacific Situation Assessment Team deployed to Manila after the kidnappings. These contingency plans, coupled with the new orders, led to the inception of OEF-P during late 2001 and early 2002 (Briscoe, 2004).

This chapter assesses OEF-P as a benchmark case of MIW for several reasons. Of primary importance is the fact that the operation is being conducted in an archipelago environment in which we would expect maritime forces to play a large role. It also includes irregular

---

[1] The ASG perpetrated another major kidnapping of 21 people, including ten Western tourists, from the Malaysian resort of Sipadan in April 2000. The hostages were taken to an ASG base in Jolo, Sulu. Most were released between August and September 2000, largely due to mediation by Libya and that country's offer of $25 million in "development aid" ("Philippine Hostages Head for Libya," 2000; FAS, 2006).

forces and tactics on both sides of the conflict. Moreover, the primary enemy in this case (ASG) uses maritime methods to a significant extent. Therefore, the operation appears on the surface to be a model case of MIW. The operation is largely considered a successful case of COIN and CT conducted by U.S. forces. However, upon closer examination, the OEF-P case reflects the strategic, operational, and tactical challenges of MIW as well as its potential benefits.

This chapter presents five main findings, three of which are specific to MIW and two of which have implications for both MIW specifically and for IW operations more broadly. First, because maritime force is generally considered to play a supportive role to ground forces in IW, it has the potential to be underutilized even in IW operations occurring in a predominantly maritime environment. Second, there is great potential for maritime-based CMOs in IW campaigns with a significant maritime component. Third, while sea-basing can be expensive, maritime operations in IW can allow the United States to scale its level of involvement, providing a military option when host-nation sensitivities or U.S. preferences constrain the deployment of U.S. ground forces. Fourth, when pursuing BPC in either MIW or land-based IW, it is important to manage strategic expectations with realistic assessments of the partner's capabilities. Finally, the OEF-P case indicates that BPC in both MIW and land-based IW should include efforts by the United States to provide equipment and technology that the partner will be able to maintain and operate without difficulty.

The remainder of this chapter considers each of these points. We focus first on the context and background of the OEF-P case, then review the specifically maritime aspects of the case, and, finally, make strategic, operational, and tactical observations regarding the case.

Background and Context

Relevant Actors

A number of actors have been involved in several longstanding conflicts in the Philippines. Of greatest concern to the United States is the ASG, which was created in the late 1980s by Filipino mujahedeen returning from and radicalized by the Soviet war in Afghanistan. Ustadz Abdurajak Janjalani founded the ASG as part of his desire to form an Iran-inspired Islamic state in the southern Philippines that would be free of non-Muslims (Guerrero, 2002, p. 15).

Of lesser concern to U.S. interests in the area is the Moro Islamic Liberation Front (MILF), which was formed in the late 1970s by the then–vice chairman of the Moro National Liberation Front (MNLF). The MILF shared the MNLF's goal of the "liberation of the homeland of Philippine Muslims from the Philippine state," but emphasized the incorporation of Islam as the basis for any political action (McKenna, 1998, pp. 155–157; Abuza, 2003, pp. 39–40). The MILF has since taken over the MNLF's position as the largest separatist organization and has, alternately, negotiated and fought with the Philippine government (Patty, 2007, p. 2). The MILF worked primarily on parallel aims to those of the MNLF, with an emphasis on incorporating Islam as the basis of any political action (Palilonis, 2009, p. 5).

Both the ASG and MILF established ties in the early 1990s with al Qaeda and the Indonesian terrorist group Jemaah Islamiyah, which was responsible for the Bali bombings in 2002 and 2005. Due to these ties, Saudi Arabian charities donated money to the two groups, and al Qaeda members established training camps for MILF, ASG, and Jemaah Islamiyah fighters in the southern Philippines (Abuza, 2003, pp. 453, 464–465). Moreover, evidence has shown that terrorist groups in the Philippines provided sanctuary in the 1990s to both the coordinator of the 1993 World Trade Center bombing (Ramzi Yousef) and the principal planner of the September 11 attacks (Khalid Sheikh Mohammed) (Palilonis, 2009, p. 6; Boot and Bennett, 2009, p. 23).

Finally, the AFP has been fighting a communist insurgency against the New People's Army for several decades. The New People's Army is the military wing of the Maoist-leaning Communist Party of the Philippines, and the AFP tends to see this fight as its primary activity (Palilonis, 2009, p. 13–14; Karniol, 2008). Because this counterinsurgency campaign is a high priority for the AFP but unrelated to U.S. objectives in the region, some have argued that it could distract the AFP from its efforts to counter the ASG. Such distractions could, in turn, leave the AFP unable to sustain the fight against the ASG on its own, without U.S. assistance (Palilonis, 2009, pp. 13–14).

U.S. Strategic Objectives

The United States' main goal in OEF-P is to build the capacity of the Philippine military to defeat terrorist organizations operating in the region. According to the Joint Special Operations Task Force–Philippines (JSOTF-P) mission statement,

> The mission of the U.S. Joint Special Operations Task Force–Philippines (JSOTF-P) is to support the comprehensive approach of the Armed Forces of the Philippines (AFP) in their fight against terrorism in the southern Philippines. At the request of the Government of the Philippines, JSTOF-P works alongside the AFP to defeat terrorists and create the conditions necessary for peace, stability, and prosperity. (JSOTF-P Public Affairs, 2009)

JSOTF-P's efforts to build AFP capacity have focused on the ASG (Palilonis, 2009).

Operational Context

As shown in Figure 3.1, OEF-P operations are conducted in the Autonomous Region of Muslim Mindanao (ARMM) on Mindanao Island. Officially established on August 1, 1989, the region has been the traditional homeland of Muslim Filipinos since the 15th century. The ARMM covers a total of 12,288 kilometers and includes the Philippines' predominantly Muslim provinces: Basilan (except Isabela City), Lanao del Sur, Maguindanao, Sulu, and Tawi-Tawi, as well as the Islamic city of Marawi. It is the only region in the Philippines that has its own government. The ARMM spans the Mindanao mainland and the Sulu Archipelago, with Lanao del Sur, Maguindanao, and Shariff Kabunsuan on the mainland and Basilan, Sulu, and Tawi-Tawi in the Sulu Archipelago (T. Wilson, 2009). Despite its autonomy, the ARMM receives a majority of its operating revenue from the Philippine national government and has yet to create significant, viable sources of additional revenue. Consequently, the ARMM is one of the country's poorest regions (Senase, 2008).

Figure 3.1
OEF-P Joint Operations Area

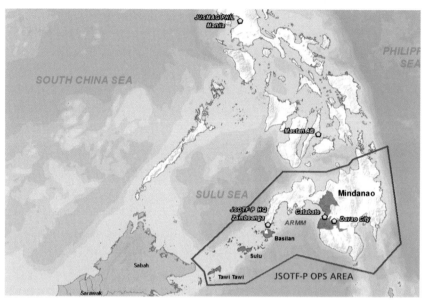

The operational environment of the Philippines is largely maritime, with more than 7,000 islands and islets and approximately 36,000 kilometers of coastline. The Sulu Archipelago stretches more than 200 nautical miles from Zamboanga to the Saba coast of Malaysia. This string of islands in the ARMM is characterized by predominantly jungle terrain, with steep interior topography. Therefore, roads are often less reliable than maritime routes, indicating that tactical and operational advantages could accrue from a maritime-focused military strategy to defeat insurgents and terrorists in the region (Briscoe, 2004; JSOTF-P Public Affairs, 2009).

In this archipelago environment, the operational context for OEF-P is broadly characterized as low-threat and semi-permissive (author discussions with NSW subject-matter experts, Cebu, Philippines, 2009).[2] In OEF-P, the United States has partnered with the Government of the Republic of the Philippines (GRP) and the AFP to build GRP and AFP capacity to defeat terrorism, as outlined above. The AFP is predominantly army-led, with an auxiliary coastal navy, a fledgling air force, and a small marine corps. At the onset of OEF-P, the Philippine Navy had just over 30 patrol gunboats, or corvettes, in various stages of operability and maintenance. Its primary vessels are 22 78-foot patrol craft fast (also known as swift boats), as well as several small amphibious LSTs (landing ships, tank) and landing craft, a Philippine Naval Special Operations Group, a small air group, and a support group (GlobalSecurity.org, 2011b).

Maritime Operations in OEF-P

The U.S.-GRP Mutual Defense Treaty was never invoked for use against the irregular threat posed by the ASG in the ARMM, and the Philippine Constitution limits U.S. military forces from engaging in any direct combat operations in OEF-P (Mutual Defense Treaty Between the United States and the Republic of the Philippines, 1951). Moreover, at the time of the operation's inception in 2001–2002, then-President Gloria Macapagal-Arroyo "insisted the U.S. military role should be advisory" (Niksch, 2003, p. 8). After a small team of U.S. joint military officers conducted a three-month assessment of requirements and plans, the U.S. Special Operation Command, Pacific, Joint Task Force (JTF) 510 deployed to Zamboanga in Mindanao. However, in view of Philippine political concerns, this force was limited to

---

[2] The ASG threat comprises a loosely organized militia with separatist objectives primarily equipped with small arms and, occasionally, explosives or a rocket-propelled grenade (RPG). The group has had intermittent and inconsistent ties with the larger MILF; however, even if those ties were closer, the ASG's rudimentary capabilities would still constitute a low-level threat. In addition, analysts describe the population in the southern Philippines (the OEF-P joint operations area) as semi-permissive because although AFP and U.S. forces can move freely for the most part, they are threatened by improvised explosive devices, ambushes, and hostile agents among the population.

600 personnel in the joint operations area (Niksch, 2003; Briscoe, 2004; Clark, Kelley, and Bummara, 2010).

This cap on the number of U.S. forces has substantially limited U.S. operational efforts to advise and assist the AFP. Such limits on U.S. troop levels effectively constrain U.S. commanders' choices as to the mix of land, air, and sea-based forces to employ. Because the mission's primary effort is to build AFP capacity, JTF-510 deployed 150 U.S. Army Special Forces troops in January 2002 to train, advise, and assist AFP soldiers in Mindanao and on Basilan Island. It also sent 450 support personnel to Edwin Andrews Air Base on Zamboanga and 50 personnel and helicopters to Mactan Air Base in Cebu. The additional 50 personnel in Cebu were allowed because they were deployed outside the joint operations area. Of these 650 personnel, fewer than 20 were from the U.S. Navy, and those personnel deployed with only two ten-meter rigid-hull inflatable boats (RIBs). Consequently, maritime operations in support of OEF-P were very limited during the operation's first two years (Niksch, 2003; Briscoe, 2004). That maritime operations were so limited in this archipelago setting demonstrates the extent to which conceptions of IW are primarily focused on land-based operations, as noted in Chapter Two.

Interestingly, however, a few maritime operations did occur early on in OEF-P, though they did not constitute major elements of the overall operational plan. Two other maritime forces were deployed to the region during those first two years, neither of which was counted against the force cap. From April to July 2002, a 340-strong naval construction task group landed on Basilan Island from the USS *Germantown* (LSD-42). For three months, the task group built bridges and landing zones; repaired a pier, an airfield, and 80 kilometers of roads; and drilled three wells. In this case, the expeditionary task group did not count against the force cap because it conducted CMOs (Niksch, 2003; Briscoe, 2004). CMOs, in general, have been largely successful in winning civilian support in OEF-P, but these efforts, a combination of subject-matter expert exchanges and civil affairs projects totaling more than $6.5 million, have been largely land-based (Puello and Smith, 2007). This has been true even for the majority of maritime-enabled CMOs. However, given the aim of such operations—to win the "hearts and minds" of the population—and the Filipino population's focus on earning a livelihood in the maritime environment, there appears to be potential for maritime-focused CMOs in this and similar environments. This potential can also be seen in the success of maritime-focused development projects conducted in the region by the U.S. Agency for International Development (USAID).[3]

The second maritime operation in OEF-P was the three-month deployment of an amphibious assault (LPD) ship just outside GRP territorial waters during the fall of 2003. The LPD served as an afloat forward staging base in support of maritime surveillance patrols. Because the LPD remained outside GRP territorial waters, it also was not counted against the force cap (Puello and Smith, 2007; Vernon, 2008). Though the LPD's operations were limited and it achieved little, it is an example of maritime force deployed early in OEF-P.

During the first two years, JTF-510 evolved into Joint Special Operations Task Force–Philippines (JSOTF-P), which marked a more sustained training, advising, and assistance mission. Maritime operations gained in importance under JSOTF-P, particularly when the high-ranking ASG leader Abu Sabaya was killed during a maritime interdiction operation.[4] JSOTF-P also identified an operational weakness of its own in the maritime arena, as ASG leaders repeatedly eluded capture via speedboat during this period (Briscoe, 2004; "Achieving Security in the Southern Philippines," 2007).

Throughout 2004, JSOTF-P gradually increased its maritime capabilities and its roles in training, advising, and assisting the Philippine Navy. By the end of 2004, JSOTF-P had added a Mark V Special

---

[3] For instance, USAID conducted a maritime-focused development project to support the construction of an ice plant on Jolo Island. This plant coincided with the construction of a new runway in Jolo and served as most efficient point in the archipelago for fishermen to pack and ship their fish. Its construction was therefore characterized as a highly successful development project; however, because the plant was not adequately protected, it was burned down by the ASG. That the ASG targeted the plant in such a way speaks to the plant's importance in winning the population's support for the AFP and GRP. Discussions with USAID officials, USAID Office, Manila, January 2010.

[4] Abu Sabaya led the ASG when it carried out the 2001 kidnappings mentioned earlier in this chapter.

Operations Craft (Mk V SOC) detachment and more SEAL operators to train and assist Philippine forces; it also reestablished the RIB detachment.[5] Granted, the U.S. Navy Special Warfare Command (NSW) footprint was still very small—just four boats and fewer than 30 personnel—but they were accompanied by the USNS *Stockham* (T-AK 3017, a maritime prepositioning force cargo vessel) and two HH-60 helicopters to serve as an afloat forward staging base. Also during 2004, a guided missile destroyer returned for a month to support Philippine Navy maritime interdiction operations outside territorial waters, and a P-3 maritime patrol aircraft was deployed to Mactan Air Base. With these added capabilities, maritime support to AFP operations increased, training increased, and the partnership between the Philippine Navy and NSW forces improved (author discussions with NSW subject-matter experts, Cebu, Philippines, 2009; Clark, Kelley, and Bummara, 2010).

In 2005, a U.S. Navy high-speed catamaran deployed to the region for a yearlong proof of concept, which added another platform for refueling, communication, staging forces, planning, hosting quick-reaction forces, and supporting medical evacuations. As the Philippine Navy units learned how to interoperate better with their swift boats and the U.S. assets, their effectiveness gradually improved (Clark, Kelley, and Bummara, 2010).

By August 2006, U.S. and AFP elements had launched Operation Ultimatum. This six-month offensive included both ground and maritime raids specifically targeting the ASG on Mindanao and the Sulu Archipelago Islands of Basilan, Jolo, and Tawi Tawi. With U.S. assistance, AFP forces gained sufficient maritime mobility to maneuver throughout the islands and support combat operations with ISR, quick-reaction forces, insertions, and exfiltrations. According to the AFP, "by late January [2007] the continuing offensive had led to

---

[5] A RIB is a 36-foot high-speed, highly buoyant, all-weather boat specifically designed to transport a fully equipped team of eight Navy SEALs and three crew members on short-range insertion and extraction missions. It provides a short-range surface mobility platform for special operations forces insertion and extraction, coastal resupply, and coastal surveillance missions. It has a 200-nm range at 32 knots, with a top speed of 45 knots. For a full description, see GlobalSecurity.org, 2011a.

the deaths of 72 ASG members, including six senior figures, and the capture of another 28" ("Achieving Security in the Southern Philippines," 2007). Of note, the ASG's senior commander, Khaddafy Janjalani, was killed in a firefight on the coast of Jolo Island in September 2006 ("Achieving Security in the Southern Philippines," 2007).[6]

After the operational effectiveness and interoperabilty of maritime operations had been proven, JSOTF-P established Task Force Archipelago in 2007. The new task force organized all NSW forces under a single commander for maritime support throughout the operating area. This, in turn, expanded maritime coordination beyond the previous piecemeal employment of maritime force under disparate Philippine Navy task forces, facilitating the use of maritime support for all Philippine JTF-Comet units (author discussions with NSW subject-matter experts, Coronado, California, and Cebu, Philippines, 2009; author discussions with Philippine Navy senior officials, Manila, Philippines, January 2010).

In 2008, maritime operations in the region increased. The year began with another successful maritime raid that resulted in the death of ASG subcommander Abu Fatima. Then, in February, the maritime support vessel *C Champion* arrived to provide direct support to JSOTF-P. A specially modified offshore support vessel from the oil industry, the ship can support all four NSW combatant craft with four davits, and a two-story operations/habitability module added to the back can house up to 30 passengers (Clark, Kelly, and Bummara, 2010).[7] It can also transport and support AFP maritime assets. In addition to this new platform, Task Force Archipelago had more than 40 personnel, two RIBs, two Mk V SOCs, four advisory teams, the USNS *Stockham*, the P-3, and intermittent support from visiting guided missile destroyers that remained outside GRP territorial waters. By the end of 2008, the AFP had reached its highest maritime operational tempo of OEF-P (author discussions with NSW subject-matter

---

[6]   Khaddafy Janjalani was the brother of ASG founder Abdurajak Janjalani, who was killed in a police shootout in late 1998.

[7]   The *C Champion* is operated by Military Sealift Command and manned by contractor personnel.

experts, Coronado, California, and Cebu, Philippines, 2009; author discussions with Philippine Navy senior officials, Manila, Philippines, January 2010).

In 2009, the USNS *Stockham* redeployed, but the AFP maintained this higher operational tempo. Moreover, the Philippine Navy began advancing its own plans to improve maritime effectiveness in the Sulu Sea. Coast Watch South, a Philippine coastal radar surveillance plan supported by the United States and Australia, also gained approval.[8] A plan for Philippine sailors (sea marshals) to ride aboard ferries in a manner akin to air marshals on airliners, also gained approval. Meanwhile, concepts for merchant vessels used to support the Philippine Naval Special Operations Group took shape, as did proposals for new assault craft, new amphibious ships, and new communication technology (author discussions with Philippine Navy senior officials, Manila, Philippines, January 2010).

Strategic Observations

Given that OEF-P has largely been fought against an irregular enemy relying strongly on maritime routes, it is surprising at first glance that the AFP, with U.S. assistance, did not establish maritime supremacy. Rather, the AFP was wading into the jungles of Basilan, where the ASG had most of the tactical advantage. Several U.S. sailors and naval officers who served in OEF-P expressed frustration with this aspect of their deployments to the region, and, indeed, the U.S. personnel limits that restricted maritime effectiveness in the context of so much operational potential made for discouraging early tours.

However, modest strategic successes resulted from the United States' chosen strategy of BPC in OEF-P. The United States recognized the nature of its partner and deployed a joint task force that complemented the AFP's predominantly ground capabilities in a constructive manner. The limit on U.S. troop levels also constrained U.S. involve-

---

[8]   The Philippines' long-term aim with regard to Coast Watch South is to eventually integrate the system with similar systems in Indonesia and Malaysia.

ment to an appropriate level, which helped the GRP understand the need to invest and lead its own efforts against the ASG.

Moreover, because the number of U.S. maritime forces was limited in the early stages of OEF-P, the Philippine Navy was effectively prompted to take the lead in maritime operations. As a result, it gained confidence with each new month of increased maritime operational tempo. To illustrate the significance of this U.S. force limitation, consider a notional counterfactual example in which the United States would deploy a substantial maritime component to the Sulu Sea—for example, a surface action group and an amphibious expeditionary strike group. If this occurred, U.S. forces would overshadow and subdue any Philippine Navy efforts, thereby working against the overall U.S. military strategy to build the Philippine partner's capacity.

This case illustrates a few strategic implications related to MIW. The first is that operators and military planners must manage expectations to ensure that the partner's capacity is effectively strengthened in a sustainable manner. By properly scaling U.S. efforts in a way that kept the AFP both successful and in the lead, OEF-P's IW campaign encouraged development and promoted the AFP's legitimacy among the Filipino population. The personnel limits and other constraints placed on U.S. forces in OEF-P are argued to be one reason that the AFP is investing more in its navy and developing practical new capabilities for the Sulu Archipelago, such as the Coast Watch South coastal surveillance system paired with additional combatant craft.

Second, by minimizing the U.S. military footprint and visibility in the Philippines, the small maritime force deployed to build AFP and GRP capacity offered a means for the United States to provide important IW capabilities without a large U.S. commitment of ground troops. Sea-based forces in the Sulu Archipelago are mobile, responsive, and capable of supporting AFP missions in larger areas. Land-based special forces A-teams in OEF-P, on the other hand, are confined to the close proximity of their liaison coordination elements because dense jungle, steep terrain, and improvised explosive devices limit their mobility from ashore bases. This case therefore suggests that MIW capabilities could be useful in future situations elsewhere in the world in which U.S. or host-nation interests constrain the commitment of U.S. troops on the ground.

Operational Observations

The operational level of the OEF-P campaign is critical in identifying the types of U.S. MIW activities that are most effective in certain scenarios. Therefore, the analysis in this section examines OEF-P operations in terms of the three types of MIW activities discussed in Chapter Two: external operations, BPC, and internal operations.

External Operations: A Supporting Effort

Chapter Two highlighted three types of MIW operational activities; of these, external operations constitute the activity requiring the least amount of direct U.S. involvement with the population ashore and consist of containment and similar strategies aimed at preventing a threat from spreading without direct U.S. military involvement. OEF-P's most pronounced operational weakness was its early failure to exploit the potential of maritime external operations: with the ASG massed on Basilan Island, U.S. and AFP forces could have worked together and deployed a modest maritime surveillance screen with maritime interdiction teams on standby, blockaded the island, and isolated the ASG. Operationally, this would have been a sensible approach.

However, the AFP has gradually developed its maritime capacity as the campaign has progressed. Whether that development is motivated by its early failures to interdict ASG fighters fleeing Basilan is unknown, but as U.S. forces increased maritime BPC efforts with more advisory teams, more combatant craft, afloat forward staging bases, and maritime patrol craft, the Philippine Navy increased its maritime operational tempo and effectiveness. As a result, the Philippine Navy has been able to more frequently deny the ASG's freedom of maneuver at sea. It has also seen more success in maritime interdiction operations in which the AFP is at a tactical advantage over the ASG.[9]

Building Partner Capacity: The Primary Effort in OEF-P

As noted in Chapter Two, BPC is a MIW operational activity that requires moderately direct involvement with the population ashore and includes training and advising the partner to build its own military capabilities. BPC was the main operational effort in OEF-P and was effective in its structured, formal training courses, robust practical exercises, and adviser teams at the tactical commander level. The comprehensive U.S. BPC effort has succeeded in developing capable leadership among Filippino officers and noncommissioned officers in the Philippine Navy and AFP for the past several years.

Moreover, as discussed earlier, equipping and training the AFP with technology and tactics that fit its requirements has been a successful approach. In addition, decisions to provide advisers who can coach the partner forces through unfamiliar communication procedures, air coordination, fire support, medical evacuation, refueling, and other joint maritime tactics have resulted in operational progress.

Internal Operations: A Supporting Effort

Finally, internal operations—as noted in Chapter Two—are those operational activities requiring the most direct level of U.S. force involvement. As with U.S. BPC activities in OEF-P, the maritime assistance U.S. forces provided the AFP is an important part of OEF-P's success. U.S. forces provided enough help to keep the AFP progressing and gaining confidence, but not so much as to undermine the AFP's legitimacy and role as the lead military force. With supporting operations that include ISR, maritime escorts, refueling, staging bases, medical evacuation, communication, and CMOs, U.S. forces have succeeded in maintaining a low profile with internal operations that quietly support the AFP's increasingly aggressive pursuit of the ASG.

---

[9]   Nonetheless, members of the Philippine Navy admitted in interviews with the authors in January 2009 that the ASG had access to faster boats and that this was a hindrance to the effectiveness of interdiction operations.

Because these supporting operations have been conducted within the joint operations area and among the population, it has been necessary for them to remain limited and discreet in order to be effective.

Tactical Observations

In the context of the chosen strategy of BPC, OEF-P illustrates important lessons about training, equipping, and advising partner forces at the tactical level. Because of the Philippines' minimal military-industrial infrastructure and its navy's small training budget, it has been necessary for U.S. forces to pass along equipment and teach tactics that are low-tech, low-cost, practical, reliable, and easy to maintain. For example, Philippine Navy sailors benefit more from learning how to operate basic radios that they can continue to use when U.S. forces leave than they would from being equipped with and trained to use encrypted satellite communication equipment. Sustainable equipment and training for the partner, in this case, consists of small combatant craft, outboard motors, very high-frequency and high-frequency radios, nautical charts, compasses, surface radars, small arms, and basic seamanship tools, all of which the Philippine Navy would reasonably be able to repair and could afford to maintain.

However, one problem associated with BPC and the allocation of rudimentary equipment is that U.S. sailors may never have been trained or may have forgotten how to use such equipment themselves. For example, U.S. sailors accustomed to Global Positioning System (GPS) navigation and forward-looking infrared systems on their RIBs may not be able to teach small-boat tactical night navigation with a compass and nautical charts. Sailors tasked with BPC may need refresher training in basic skills and tactics. In addition, personnel advising partner forces should ideally have foreign language skills and training to ensure effective communication with partner forces. Because U.S. Navy sailors currently have skills and abilities that are geared toward complex, sophisticated systems, future research might examine how the training of U.S. Navy personnel could be modified in an era of increasing MIW.

Another equipment-related problem in the context of BPC has been evident in the United States' gifting of old or obsolete equipment to the Philippine Navy, which creates problems when trying to access spare parts. In many cases, the Philippine Navy has managed to build its own spare parts, but it is worthwhile to note that this is a challenge facing partnering nations that do not have equal technical capabilities and types of equipment (author discussions with Philippine Navy personnel, January 2009). Notably, this problem is not contained to BPC among maritime forces: the Philippine Air Force faces a similar problem with equipment received from its U.S. partner.

Each of the observations identified in this chapter speaks to key issues pertaining specifically to the OEF-P case. To what extent can these findings be generalized to other instances of MIW? The next chapter assesses a broader spectrum of MIW cases to derive lessons that are applicable across a range of MIW scenarios and to point out ways in which the OEF-P case may or may not be an anomalous example of MIW.

CHAPTER FOUR

A Comparative Historical Analysis of Maritime Irregular Warfare

As Chapter Three illustrated, the OEF-P case of MIW includes various tactical, operational, and strategic lessons. This chapter examines and compares a variety of other MIW cases, seeking to derive additional lessons regarding MIW. The remainder of this chapter explores MIW cases across the spectrum of strategic scenarios presented in Chapter Two, looking first at MIW in COIN, then assessing MIW in UW, and finally turning to MIW in law-enforcement scenarios.

Strategic Scenario 1: Counterinsurgency in Vietnam

The United States and its allies have a fairly extensive historical track record of using maritime forces in COIN missions, a trend that continues today. Maritime forces were used in COIN operations in three of the cases we examined: Operations Market Time, Game Warden, Coronado, and Sealords in the Vietnam War; U.S. and Colombian maritime operations as part of Plan Colombia; and (as noted in Chapter Three) OEF-P. In each of these cases, maritime forces played a vital support role to ground forces and, again, were tactically successful on many counts. Recognition of the value of maritime capabilities for COIN functions is increasingly important, as insurgents themselves are conducting offensive maritime irregular operations against established powers with increasing frequency, often successfully. An example of this phenomenon is the Sea Tigers wing of the LTTE in Sri Lanka, a case explored in greater depth in the next chapter. Here we examine maritime COIN operations in Vietnam, and we focus on the CT and law-enforcement aspects of the Colombia case in the next section.

When compared to the analysis of OEF-P in the previous chapter, it becomes clear that both the Vietnam and Philippine cases reveal the potential of maritime forces to contribute substantially to COIN operations and point to possible ways in which their use might benefit the United States and its allies in such contingencies in the future. Particularly significant is the suggestion that, because COIN operations still tend to occur in sensitive political environments, the minimal footprint and low visibility offered by maritime operations can provide a strategic advantage to the United States and its allies when used in conjunction with ground-based COIN operations.

Maritime Operations in the Vietnam War: Operations Market Time, Game Warden, Coronado, and Sealords

The U.S. military utilized maritime capabilities in a number of operations during the Vietnam War, targeting the coastal and riverine supply routes of the Viet Cong (VC) guerrillas as well as striking directly at major VC formations with infantry and artillery deployed from specialized assault boats. These operations employed units and personnel from the Army, Navy, and Coast Guard and drew on a range of new and innovative riverine assault tactics developed by amphibious warfare and special operations experts from all three services (Fulton, 1985).

MIW efforts against the VC were concentrated in the Mekong Delta region in South Vietnam from 1965 to 1971. This region included fully one-quarter of South Vietnam's land area and hosted a population of 8 million in 1965 (about half of the country's total population) (Fulton, 1985, p. 17). The area was South Vietnam's agricultural breadbasket and could not be allowed to fall into the hands of the VC. However, by 1965, the VC was starting to choke off shipments of rice from the Mekong Delta to the national capital, Saigon, and U.S. military leaders at U.S. Military Assistance Command, Vietnam (MACV), headquarters began to plan for a more aggressive U.S. posture in the Delta to meet this new threat. MACV was the unified command structure for all U.S. military forces in South Vietnam during the war. It was created on February 8, 1962, in response to increased U.S. involvement in Vietnam and was disbanded on March 29, 1973 (Stanton, 1986; Sorley, 2007).

There were four distinct U.S. maritime IW campaigns in South Vietnam. Operation Market Time was a U.S. Navy effort to stop troops and supplies intended to support VC forces from flowing by sea between North and South Vietnam. Operation Game Warden was a riverine operation that used river-patrol boats to disrupt VC supply traffic on the major rivers of the Mekong Delta. Both Market Time and Game Warden were external operations, as defined in Chapter Two. The Coronado series of operations used the combined-arms Mobile Riverine Force (MRF) to directly attack VC sanctuaries and base areas in the Mekong Delta and represented the most ambitious and aggressive U.S. maritime campaign during the Vietnam War. Thus, Coronado was a series of internal operations, according to the definition provided in Chapter Two. Operation Sealords, which took place during the last phase of U.S. military involvement in the Mekong Delta, was a combination of both external and internal operations. It was an effort to mount a comprehensive U.S.–South Vietnamese riverine campaign that included the interception of VC river supply traffic, the pacification of some towns and villages, the establishment of permanent waterway interdiction barriers near the Cambodian border, and strike operations against major VC formations.

Operation Market Time was clearly a success, but the other three campaigns achieved somewhat mixed results. While the Game Warden and Coronado efforts did weaken the VC in the Mekong Delta and heavily degraded the VC infrastructure, they did not decisively defeat the insurgents before U.S. public opinion turned against the war in 1968–1969 and forced a military withdrawal from South Vietnam.[1] Operation Sealords did make substantial progress in reducing VC mar-

---

[1]   In addition to the degrading effects of these riverine operations on the VC infrastructure, it is also worth noting that the military and political infrastructure was decimated by operations, also targeting the cadres, that were conducted by Game Warden SEALs and other SEALs attached to Provincial Reconnaissance Units in the classified Phoenix program. Hanoi, not without difficulty, then had to replace the eliminated southern cadres with northerners, and it took time for these new cadres to be accepted and adapt (Andrade, 1990, pp. 276–277).

itime traffic in the last years of U.S. military involvement, but it did not succeed in fully preparing the South Vietnamese army and navy to secure the delta on their own in the absence of U.S. assistance.

Overview of MIW Operations in Vietnam

U.S. maritime efforts in Vietnam commenced after the February 1965 Vung Ro Bay incident, in which a trawler was intercepted landing arms and ammunition for the VC in Khanh Hoa Province. This incident revealed to U.S. commanders the extent of the flow of arms and ammunition from North Vietnam via the South China Sea to VC units in the Mekong Delta region. U.S. forces quickly responded with the Market Time campaign of interdictions by Navy destroyers, ocean minesweepers, swift boats, Navy patrol gunboats, and U.S. Coast Guard cutters (Bassett, 2006, pp. 5–6). Market Time was quite successful. In his memoirs, MACV commander General William C. Westmoreland wrote that, whereas the VC received 70 percent of their supplies via the South China Sea route in 1965, by the end of 1966, only 10 percent of their supplies were arriving by this route (Westmoreland, 1976).

To compensate for this squeeze on coastal supply lines, the VC came to depend ever more on bringing supplies into the Mekong Delta from Cambodia and then distributing them via the delta's vast network of rivers, streams, and canals with small boats, barges, and junks. In response to this shift, the United States mounted Operation Game Warden in December 1965. Game Warden was a riverine interdiction operation with the aim of disrupting VC supply traffic on the main rivers and waterways of the Mekong Delta. During the operation, 120 U.S. river-patrol boats searched 2,000 junks and sampans each day in the Mekong Delta region; not only did this effort cut down on the supply flow to VC main force units, but it also hampered VC tax collection in the delta (Westmoreland, 1976, pp. 184–185). Army combat helicopters provided cover for the swift boat crews, providing an early demonstration of the importance of combined-arms tactics in riverine warfare.

However, by mid-1966, U.S. commanders came to believe that the only way to eradicate the VC from the Mekong Delta was to use U.S. ground forces to strike at the base areas deep in the region that the VC's main units used to organize, train, and equip their forces. The U.S. commanders understood that Game Warden river interdiction alone could not fully defeat the VC. Thus, from February 1967 to July 1968, the focus of operations in the region was the Coronado series of strikes with ground forces. Coronado was an 18-month campaign aimed at destroying the major VC base areas in the Mekong Delta using highly kinetic operations involving both riverine boats and helicopters to move Army infantry.

The centerpiece of Coronado was the MRF, which was made up of the U.S. Navy's River Assault Flotilla One and the 2nd Brigade of the Army's 9th Infantry Division. The MRF employed innovative new systems in its operations, including barge mounted 105-mm howitzers for mobile firepower along the delta's rivers, armored troop carriers to move infantry assault teams to their targets, and a series of afloat bases for MRF personnel that were constructed by modifying LSTs (Fulton, 1985, Chapter 4). As noted earlier, Coronado also featured the large-scale use of heliborne infantry assaults as a complement to the movement of infantry by armored boats. In fact, the most effective attacks in Coronado were those in which riverborne infantry pushed VC units directly toward defensive positions held by rapidly and precisely deployed heliborne infantry units (i.e., the "hammer and anvil" approach).

Despite the many U.S. technological and tactical innovations employed in Coronado, the VC were able to counter with their own innovations, including combat swimmers armed with mines who attacked U.S. afloat bases and carefully synchronized RPG ambushes of armored troop carrier convoys. Overall, though, the MRF did deal heavy blows to the VC forces in the Mekong Delta. Unfortunately, Coronado did not turn out to be a decisive success because the numerous U.S. strike operations were not quickly followed up with any systematic pacification campaign aimed at the civilian population (Fulton, 1985, Chapter 9). The pacification efforts that began later under the auspices of Operation Sealords were too little, too late, as the United States was already withdrawing from the delta by the time Sealords was under way.

Operation Sealords began in October 1968, in the aftermath of the Tet Offensive, as a joint operation between U.S. and South Vietnamese forces and was completely turned over to the South Vietnamese military by 1971. It was designed to be a comprehensive campaign that incorporated river interdiction, pacification, and strike operations in a single, large-scale effort. In support of the operation, the U.S. Navy's Coastal Surveillance Force deployed 81 swift boats, 24 Coast Guard patrol cutters, and 39 other vessels. Meanwhile, the Navy's River Patrol Force operated 258 patrol and minesweeping boats and a 3,700-strong riverine assault force that included 184 armored monitors and transport carriers. Finally, the United States added in a light-attack helicopter squadron and five SEAL platoons to the Sealords force roster. The operation succeeded in securing transportation routes, cutting some infiltration routes from Cambodia, and establishing an almost uninterrupted patrolled waterway interdiction barrier from Tay Ninh to the Gulf of Siam (McQuilkin, 1997; Paluso, 2002).

Key Insights

One can glean three major insights from the Vietnam MIW case. First, this case shows that coastal maritime interdiction can play an instrumental role in setting the conditions for success in IW by cutting the supply lines that sustain an insurgency. This comports with previous research on COIN showing that the presence or absence of sanctuary for the insurgents is a key variable determining success (Gompert and Gordon, 2008). As such, maritime approaches can become an important domain of IW as insurgents work to keep open and exploit sea lines of communication and counterinsurgents seek to disrupt those lines and use them to support their own mobility and logistics. In the Vietnam operations examined here, coastal interdiction was easier to conduct than either riverine or ground interdiction when enough ISR assets and naval platforms were devoted to the task on a constant basis. Operation Market Time was the biggest maritime success story for the United States in the Vietnam War and, if not for the option of shifting their supply routes from the South China Sea to the rivers that flow from Cambodia into the Mekong Delta, it is likely that the VC would have had to give up on its insurgency campaign in the region.

However, when compared to OEF-P, it becomes clear that geography plays a major role in determining the level of ease with which such interdiction operations may be conducted. Much of South Vietnam's coastline is oriented from north to south and approached from the east, so a sea barrier oriented from north to south and facing east could be effective in that context. The Sulu Archipelago, in contrast, has numerous islands and islets, each surrounded by 360-degree coastlines and each providing a surveillance shadow for others. Numerous vessels are engaged in fishing and interisland transportation in this region, and all would have to be stopped and searched during an interdiction campaign. In the context of the Philippines and similarly situated regions, therefore, maritime interdiction may be vastly more challenging than it was along the coast of Vietnam.

Second, the Vietnam experience shows that in riverine COIN, just as in land-based COIN, strike operations against the main insurgent units have to be followed up by efforts to enhance local public support for the mission if victory is to be achieved. The primary weakness of the Coronado campaign in 1967–1968 was that it did not exploit the defeats inflicted upon VC main force units with a rapid and comprehensive effort to enhance public support throughout the Mekong Delta. This allowed the insurgency to survive in the region.

Finally, the Vietnam case tells us that riverine MIW benefits from a combined-arms approach. The United States was able to degrade VC main force units in the delta in the late 1960s by employing closely coordinated riverborne and heliborne infantry, with all infantry attacks backed up by barge-mounted artillery and attack helicopters. The Army-Navy combined-arms team that was assembled under the auspices of the MRF attacked the VC across many dimensions simultaneously, giving the insurgents very few options for effective defense when they were caught operating in large formations. Although the VC fought back against major U.S. assaults, in almost every case they were eventually overwhelmed by the combined-arms approach. Thus, as Coronado and Sealords progressed, the VC had to rely increasingly on ambushes conducted by small units to maintain viability in the Mekong Delta region.

Strategic Scenario 2: Maritime Support to Law Enforcement in Counterterrorism and Counternarcotics Operations in Colombia and to Counterpiracy Operations off the Horn of Africa

The fact that MIW operations have occurred in COIN situations to a significant extent in recent years is not surprising, given the current prominence of COIN in U.S. military strategy and IW doctrine. IW contingencies with a significant reliance on law enforcement are similarly prevalent both in doctrine and practice, with many recent instances of MIW falling into this category. Examples of such cases include CN and CT operations in Colombia and CP operations off the HoA.[2]

Counternarcotics and Counterterrorism Operations in Colombia

In a manner similar to U.S.-supported COIN activities in OEF-P, CN and CT operations as part of Plan Colombia have been scaled primarily as a BPC mission, which allows the Colombian military to take the upper hand while the United States provides funding, training, weapons, and equipment. As in the previously discussed cases, Plan Colombia entails maritime operations, mainly in support of ground and air operations. Maritime operations include both coastal and riverine activities to support two interrelated goals—interdiction of drugs and supplies and maritime support to law enforcement—both of which are efforts to counter ongoing threats posed by terrorists, insurgents, and drug traffickers.

Colombia's jungle topography, with a dense canopy, swamps, and mangroves near river basins connected to the sea, has provided haven for various paramilitary and revolutionary forces for decades. The most continually problematic of these organizations is the leftist Revolutionary Armed Forces of Colombia (FARC). Others have his-

---

[2]   We recognize that CT and COIN are often linked and that, for instance, one could assess the COIN aspects of the Colombia case just as easily as one could assess its CT aspects. We focus here on the CT and CN elements of the Colombia case in an effort to identify insights that are specifically relevant to CT and CN operations in MIW, since several of our other examples include analyses of COIN in maritime environments.

torically included the leftist National Liberation Army (ELN) and the United Self-Defense Groups of Colombia, which are now reemerging as autonomous criminal bands (*bandas criminales*) known as "Bacrim" (author interviews with Colombian police personnel, Bogota, Colombia, March 2009; author interviews with U.S. officials, Washington, D.C., January 2009; Webb-Vidal, 2009; McDermott, 2010).

To counter these threats, then–Colombian President Andres Pastrana Arango initiated Plan Colombia with the United States in 2000, merging CT and CN efforts in the hopes of ending the Colombian government's long-standing armed conflict, eliminating drug trafficking, depriving the FARC of crucial operational income derived from the drug trade, and promoting economic and social development. Because Colombia had replaced Peru and Bolivia as the primary source of coca production by 1998, the United States devoted $4.5 billion to Plan Colombia between FY 2000 and FY 2005 in an effort to prevent the flow of illegal drugs into the United States and to help the Colombian government promote peace while simultaneously contributing to South American regional security (Marcella, 2001; U.S. Senate Committee on Foreign Relations, 2005). By 2008, the U.S. Government Accountability Office reported that the United States had provided more than $6 billion in military and nonmilitary assistance to Colombia through the initiative (GAO, 2008). In 2008 alone, Colombia received $541 million, and it received another $540 million in Plan Colombia funds in 2009. The United States reportedly invested between $511 million and $530 million in Plan Colombia in 2010 (Alsema, 2009).

Despite the financial breadth of U.S. assistance to Colombia, Congress originally capped U.S. troop levels in the country at 500 and prohibited the presence of any more than 300 U.S. contract personnel in the country (Miller, 2001). The total number of U.S. military personnel in Colombia nearly doubled following the passage of the 2005 Defense Authorization Act, which called for 800 U.S. troops and 600 U.S. civilian contractors to be deployed there ("U.S. to Double Military in Colombia," 2004). Nonetheless, U.S. legislators clearly limited the number of troops that the United States could deploy to Colombia; Plan Colombia operations are therefore largely oriented toward building the capacity of the Colombian military. In the presence of legal limitations on U.S. troop deployment to this theater, maritime forces have an advantage in being able to do more with fewer troops than is possible with ground forces.

Indeed, while the vast majority of Plan Colombia funding supports land operations, the Colombian and U.S. militaries (as well as private contractors hired as part of Plan Colombia) also conduct operations in the air and in maritime environments ("Fighting One Half of the Drug War: Colombia," 2009).[3] Land operations are aimed at training and providing security assistance to the Colombian military and police forces to enable them to break up rebel strongholds and provide security for Colombian civilians, but they also include ground interdiction operations (U.S. Department of State, Bureau of Western Hemisphere Affairs, 2001). Air operations comprise air support to the overall mission and coca eradication operations, a large portion of which are conducted by private contractors (Kraul, 2009). Maritime operations, meanwhile, include both coastal and riverine activities to support two interrelated goals: interdiction and maritime support to law enforcement. These activities therefore primarily serve to support land-based activities, as tends to be the case with MIW activities.

Maritime Interdiction Activities

Although they serve a supportive role to ground operations, in many ways, maritime interdiction activities make a significant contribution to CN efforts off Colombia's shores. Maritime interdiction is crucial in this context, as a majority of Colombia's total cocaine exports leave the country by sea from the Pacific coast. While most narcotics exports leave Colombia via "go-fast" speedboats, they are increasingly being transported aboard self-propelled semi-submersibles (SPSSs) as well (Allen, 2008; Harwood, 2009; Ishani and Manfredi, 2009; U.S. Department of State, Bureau of International Narcotics and Law

---

[3] For instance, of the $519.2 million in U.S. aid for the Colombian military in 2001, 80 percent funded a ground offensive "push" into southern Colombia, led by three CN battalions trained by U.S. special forces personnel. The remainder went to fund national, air, river, and ground interdiction operations along with military human rights training and military justice reforms.

Enforcement Affairs, 2010).[4] The United States now provides "midnight express" boats, effective in chasing down the go-fast boats, to the Colombian Coast Guard (author interviews with Colombian Coast Guard officials, Cartagena, Colombia, November 2008, and Bogota, Colombia, March 2009).

Shipments aboard semi-submersibles are much less easy to interdict (Harwood, 2009, pp. 1–2).[5] According to the State Department's *2010 International Narcotics Control Strategy Report*, SPSSs may have hauled 423 metric tons of cocaine in 2008 alone. It is estimated that only 71 metric tons of that combined load were prevented from reaching the market, with U.S. Coast Guard interdictions accounting for 56.3 metric tons of that total (Harwood, 2009, p. 2). Detection of SPSSs in the open ocean is extremely difficult, as the bulk of the vessel is submerged and able to evade most radar. Further complicating efforts to catch SPSSs is the fact that crews tend to scuttle the vessels after each drop-off. Generally, the crew loads the cargo onto a Mexican drug-trafficking ship, sinks the SPSS, boards the Mexican ship, and is taken to somewhere along Mexico's western coast. While the range of adversary capabilities that the United States will likely face in future MIW operations is explored in greater depth in Chapter Five, it is relevant to note here that—because they are so difficult to detect once they reach the open sea—semi-submersibles demonstrate how an adaptive and technically proficient irregular enemy can pose an immense challenge to maritime forces in IW (Ishani and Manfredi, 2009).[6] Furthermore,

---

[4] Estimates of the amount of cocaine exported through maritime means range from 55 to 90 percent of Colombia's total cocaine exports.

[5] An SPSS is a motor-propelled, flat-decked vessel with a pilothouse rising only about 18 inches above the waterline. It ranges from 30 to 80 feet long and is able to carry between four and 12 metric tons of cocaine in a single load at up to 12 miles per hour. These vessels can travel up to 2,000 miles without refueling. Early on, SPSSs were constructed of wood and fiberglass, but now they are constructed of steel hulls, armed with modern electronics to avoid detection, and equipped with GPS navigation systems to avoid the need for external communication. Believed to operate predominantly in the eastern Pacific, an SPSS was first sighted in 1993; it is unknown how many times these vessels were used before or since then.

[6] SPSSs do not leave a visible wake like go-fast boats and do not show up on most radar. Infrared systems can spot their heat signature, but the newest models have insulated motors

narcotics traffickers in Colombia have now developed the capability to construct fully submersible vessels, one of which was discovered in July 2010 ("Cocaine Submarine Seized July 2," 2010). Another, discovered in February 2011, was large enough to carry eight tons of cocaine and four crew members in its air-conditioned interior and included a small kitchen; it was able to dive up to eight meters underwater to travel all the way from Colombia to Mexico (Stone, 2011).

Indeed, the extent to which the Colombian Navy and Coast Guard are forced to play "catch-up" with a constantly innovating enemy is problematic. According Captain Mario Rodriguez, commander of the Colombian Coast Guard, "In the 1980s we were tracking and chasing cigarette boats that traveled twenty knots per hour, and soon go-fast boats with three, four, or even five engines that could go forty to fifty knots" (Ishani and Manfredi, 2009). The switch from shipping large quantities of cocaine in single consignments on fishing trawlers to a "scatter-gun" approach, in which smaller quantities are smuggled in stages up the coast on go-fast boats, was a direct reaction by the traffickers to several major drug seizures that occurred between 2002 and 2006. Moreover, as noted earlier, the traffickers continue to challenge U.S. and Colombian capabilities with their use of increasingly sophisticated semi-submersibles. Captain Rodriguez acknowledged that the SPSSs themselves have become much more modern and technically advanced over time, illustrating the innovativeness of the traffickers: "The first semi-submersibles we came across in the 1990s were very rudimentary. They didn't have a motor and were attached with a cable to fishing boats, which dragged them along to their destinations" (Ishani and Manfredi, 2009).

On an encouraging note, U.S. and Colombian forces' abilities to detect and halt narcotics shipments via SPSSs appear to be increasing, though this possibility should be assessed critically and cautiously. Between 2001 and 2006, there were 23 confirmed SPSS "incidents," broadly defined to include sightings, scuttlings, and seizures. In 2007, that number increased to 42 incidents in one year. In 2008, there were

---

that produce so little heat that surveillance planes often cannot spot them unless they are directly above them.

77 SPSS sightings (Harwood, 2009, p. 1). All in all, it has been esti-mated that the Colombian Navy has seized approximately 61 SPSSs since 1993. As of April 2011, it was reported that officials had seized 32 SPSSs over the previous decade, including 12 in 2010 alone (Uribe, 2011). These statistics may be misleading, however. As noted earlier, only 71 metric tons of cocaine shipped via SPSSs was interdicted before making it to the market in 2008—less than 20 percent of the total estimated amount (423 metric tons) shipped on these vessels that year. Moreover, an increase in the number of SPSS sightings may mean that U.S. detection capabilities are improving, or it may mean that the fre-quency of SPSS voyages is increasing, which would bode poorly for U.S. efforts to halt these shipments.

One of the tactics now practiced by Colombian forces seeking to counter the threat posed by semi- and fully submersible vessels is the early detection of SPSS and fully submersible vessel construction on Colombian territory, which illustrates that maritime forces in IW are often used in nontraditional environments (i.e., on land) as well as in the water (O'Rourke, 2010).[7] Indeed, the Colombian Navy is the main force used to search for the assembly sites of these semi-submersibles, which they deem to be one of their most challenging tasks. As a young Colombian Navy officer reported, "We sail up these muddy, narrow rivers and there is dense vegetation all around us. Many of the people who live up there are working for the traffickers. As soon as we pass, someone picks up a cell phone and lets the people upstream know that we are coming" (Ishani and Manfredi, 2009). Ambush risk is also high (Ishani and Manfredi, 2009). Despite these difficulties, the Colombian Navy has had some success in fighting SPSS construction: In 2007, its forces raided a clandestine jungle shipyard near the port of Buenaven-tura, and two SPSSs were discovered. One was ready to launch, while the other was 70-percent complete. Colombian security forces also

---

[7] This is seen, for instance, in OEF in Afghanistan. In early 2010, the U.S. Navy had 12,300 active and reserve personnel on the ground throughout the U.S. Central Command region, supporting Navy, joint force, and combatant commander requirements. Navy com-manders were leading six of the 12 U.S.-led Provincial Reconstruction Teams in Afghani-stan, and Navy SEABEE construction battalions were rebuilding schools and restoring criti-cal infrastructure.

raided at least two more construction sites in 2008 (Harwood, 2009, pp. 4–5). Meanwhile, in November 2008, Colombia's Department of Administrative Security arrested Enrique Portocarrero (aka, Captain Nemo), who was responsible for building as many as 20 fiberglass semi-submersibles (Kraul, 2008).

Riverine Support to Law Enforcement in Colombia

Beyond interdiction efforts, maritime forces pursuing the CN and CT missions in Colombia conduct riverine operations to support coastal law enforcement. The U.S. Marine Corps has stepped up its involvement in riverine CN operations, recruiting a privately contracted "riverine plans officer" in early 2006 to serve as the primary operations adviser responsible for overseeing strategic and tactical operations in and around Colombian waterways. The riverine plans officer works in line with the larger U.S. efforts to build the Colombian military's capacity, providing combat and tactical training, coordinating operations, and incorporating human rights and Geneva Convention instruction into Colombian marine corps training (Peacock, 2006).

In one example of how such riverine operations can be used to support law-enforcement activities, the Colombian Navy, with U.S. support, set up an advanced riverine post in Barrancon to patrol the Guaviare River. Reportedly, the post substantially added to the security force presence in the Guaviare region of southern Colombia ("Plan Colombia and Beyond," 2008). Currently, however, riverine and non-riverine maritime patrols have not been combined with any CMO or COIN efforts to improve the living conditions of civilians living in Colombia's coastal communities. This is a marked difference from IW operations on land in OEF-P, in which subject-matter expert exchanges and civil affairs projects totaling more than $6.5 million have been employed in a largely land-based CMO campaign that has mostly succeeded in winning the hearts and minds of Philippine civilians (Puello and Smith, 2007, p. 3). Due to the prevalence of the maritime dimension of both countries' problems with insurgents and the conspicuous underemphasis on maritime-based CMO projects, both could benefit from the enhancement of CMO efforts in the maritime arena.

Counterpiracy Operations off the Horn of Africa

Maritime CMOs to benefit coastal communities could also be added to CP operations off the HoA in an effort to develop or sustain local coastal communities in Somalia and thus remove one of the greatest incentives for piracy. Piracy off the HoA has expanded rapidly in recent years.[8] Between 2008 and 2011, 776 incidents were reported in the region, which equates to just under 50 percent (48.8 percent) of the global tally during the period (IMB, 2010a, p. 5; IMB, 2010b, p. 5, IMB, 2012, p. 5). Since 2008, more than 450 ships have been attacked in this area and over 3,500 mariners have been taken hostage (GAO, 2010, p. 1; "EU Mulls Expanding Anti-Piracy Missions to Beaches," 2011; UK House of Commons Foreign Affairs Committee, 2011, p. 16). As of January 1, 2012, pirate gangs in Somalia continued to hold 11 vessels and 193 crew members of different nationalities (IMB, 2011, p. 20; "EU Mulls Expanding Anti-Piracy Missions to Beaches," 2011). These same entities are also thought to earn upwards of $80 million in ransom payments per year (the figure in 2011 was thought to amount to $135 million), with the typical settlement in the range of $2–$4 million as of late 2011—compared to $600,000 in 2007 and $150,000 in 2005 (Bandel and Crowley, 2008; Houreld, 2010a; "Somali Pirates Obtained Over USD 135 Million in Ransoms in 2011," 2011). Syndicates have attacked all types of craft—freighters, bulk carriers, oil tankers, fishing trawlers—and have exhibited a capacity to operate far from shore. As of this writing, a vast stretch of the Indian Ocean had been designated as high risk for Somali piracy, extending from the Red Sea in the west to 76 degrees longitude in the east, 22 degrees in the south, and 21.5 degrees in the north (Bandel and Crowley, 2008; GAO, 2010, p. 1; IMB, 2010, p. 20).[9]

The rapid escalation of armed attacks off the HoA has triggered unprecedented CP action on the part of the international community. While these actions have borne some dividends, their overall utility in

---

[8] For the purposes of this chapter, the HoA includes the Gulf of Aden, the Red Sea, and the waters off Somalia.

[9] For example, in March 2010, Somali pirates hijacked the MV *Frigia* some 1,100 nm from their base in eastern Africa.

addressing Somali-sourced piracy is questionable in several respects. Moreover, they fail to take into account the principal triggers for this manifestation of unconventional maritime disorder, which stem not from the sea but from land.

International measures to address piracy have included the formation of coalition task forces, unilateral deployments, judicial agreements with third-party states to prosecute suspects, and the passage of three United Nations Security Council resolutions (UNSCRs), as discussed next.

Coalition Task Forces and Unilateral Deployments

In January 2009, U.S. Navy forces announced the creation of CTF-151 to monitor a self-defined maritime security patrol area in the Gulf of Aden, Gulf of Oman, and Arabian Gulf.[10] The CTF was to form the basis for a multinational coalition CP force. As of January 2012, CTF-151 consisted of vessels from the United States, the United Kingdom, South Korea, Singapore, Thailand, and Turkey (the current flag). A command staff, including personnel from Pakistan, Bahrain, Denmark, and Jordan, oversees these ships (Combined Maritime Forces, undated; Cummins, 2009; Hilley, 2009; author interview with a Royal Australian Navy officer, Canberra, Australia, May 2009; GAO, 2010, pp. 73–74; Gustin, 2010; "RSS Endurance to the Gulf," 2010; "Thailand Sends Two Warships to Tackle Somali Pirates," 2010).

CTF-151 complements the combined European Union Naval Force (EUNAVFOR) operation Atalanta, which was deployed in December 2008. The flotilla has a mandate that currently runs through to the end of December 2012 and consists of frigates, corvettes, aircraft, and one submarine. Contributing countries include the United Kingdom, France, Spain, Germany, Italy, Greece, Malta, the Netherlands, Sweden, Luxembourg, Belgium, Ireland, and Finland (Council of the

---

[10] Prior to the creation of CTF-151, the task of conducting maritime patrols in the Gulf of Aden fell to CTF-150, which was established at the outset of OEF in 2001. However, this flotilla was mandated only to address threats such as terrorism, drug smuggling, and weapon trafficking and had no independent authority to conduct CP operations per se. For further details, see Combined Maritime Forces, undated.

European Union, undated; "European Union to Deploy Anti-Piracy Operations Planes in the Seychelles," 2009; Boot, 2009; Greenblatt, 2009; Hansen, 2009, p. 45; author interviews with UK and EU naval and defense officials, May 2009; GAO, 2010, pp. 73–74; "President Approves Deployment to Gulf of Aden," 2010). Specific tasks slated for Atalanta include the following:

- the protection of World Food Programme vessels delivering food aid to displaced populations in Somalia
- the protection of vulnerable vessels cruising off the Somali coast
- the deterrence, prevention, and repression of acts of piracy and armed robbery off the Somali coast (Gettleman, 2008; Gortney, 2009; Hanson, 2010; Viscusi, 2009; IMB, 2010a, p. 41).

The North Atlantic Treaty Organization (NATO) has also sent vessels to the HoA. The first mission, codenamed Operation Allied Provider, was dispatched to work with Atalanta in protecting World Food Programme vessels. The current deployment, Operation Ocean Shield, commenced on August 17, 2009, and was ongoing as of this writing. In addition to undertaking CP patrols, the NATO force is assisting regional states in augmenting their own ability to conduct effective maritime surveillance and interdiction in their territorial waters ("NATO to Send New Somalia Anti-Piracy Force," 2009; NATO, 2009; Schuman, 2010). International partners currently involved in Ocean Shield include the United States, Germany, Greece, Italy, the Netherlands, Spain, Turkey, and the United Kingdom (GAO, 2010, pp. 73–74).

These coalition task forces are coordinated through Combined Maritime Forces Shared Awareness and Deconfliction (SHADE) meetings, which commenced in 2008. Apart from states participating in CTF-151, EUNAVFOR, and Ocean Shield, these interactive sessions have included personnel (on an ad hoc basis) from China, Russia, INTERPOL, and industry. Meetings are held every four to six weeks and are intended to provide a forum for militaries operating in the region to share information and best practices, as well as ensure they are working toward a common purpose. The SHADE mechanism also acts as a centralized hub that shipping companies can access to ascertain the current operating environment in the Gulf of Aden and determine where assets are deployed (author interview with a Royal Australian Navy officer, Canberra, Australia, May 2009; Contact Group on Piracy off the Coast of Somalia, 2009; GAO, 2010, p. 37).

Apart from CTF-151, EUNAVFOR, and NATO, a number of other states have sent frigates to protect or escort shipping vessels off the HoA, including India, China, Russia, Pakistan, Saudi Arabia, and Malaysia. According to the One Earth Future Foundation, around 43 ships operate off the HoA at any given time (A. Bowden et al., 2010, p. 5; see also Demick, 2008; Gettleman, 2008; Otterman and McDonald, 2008; "China to Send Fresh Anti-Piracy Navy Convoy," 2009; Gortney, 2009; IMB, 2009, p. 37; McDonald, 2009b; Viscusi, 2009; GAO, 2010, p. 22).

Judicial Agreements

On the legal front, the United States, United Kingdom, European Union, Canada, China, and Denmark have all entered into transfer accords with Kenya, whereby the latter will act as a third party to prosecute individuals suspected of engaging in armed maritime crimes. The EU and UK have comparable agreements with the Seychelles, and the EU with Mauritius. As of this writing, similar arrangements with Mozambique, Tanzania, Uganda, and South Africa were being developed (UN Secretary-General, 2010, p. 15; IMB, 2011, p. 31; UK House of Commons Foreign Affairs Committee, 2011, pp. 49–50).[11] The accords essentially reflect the uncertainties that are associated with trying maritime bandits in domestic courts. Although piracy is defined as a crime of universal jurisdiction,[12] many countries do not have the appropriate domestic legislation to actually bring perpetrators to jus-

---

[11] The main agreements are with Kenya, which was deemed a viable candidate on account of its geographic proximity to Somalia and the HoA, the existence of appropriate domestic statutes penalizing maritime crime, the country's standing security and CT cooperation with the United States and the United Kingdom, and the government's willingness to accept suspects in exchange for Western development assistance dollars.

[12] A crime of universal jurisdiction means that all sovereign states have both the right and responsibility to detain or arrest any person who is caught in the prosecution of that act.

tice. Moreover, at least some of the states contributing to CP patrols in the Gulf of Aden remain concerned about potential claims for political asylum if pirates are tried but subsequently found not guilty. Reflecting this situation, of the 1,129 pirates detained by naval forces operating off the HoA between August 2008 and June 2010, 638—almost 57 percent—were simply disarmed and released due to the difficulties of establishing a viable case that would stand up in a court of law (Boot, 2009, pp. 105–106; Chalk, Smallman, and Burger, 2009, p. 227; GAO, 2010, pp. 22–23).

The transfer agreements with Kenya, the Seychelles, and Mauritius are primarily designed to overcome this judicial void by providing prominent flag states with the option of putting pirates on land where legal consequences can be administered (Cala, 2009; Gettleman, 2009b; Gilmore, 2009). Under the accords, any signatory patrolling state or organization that apprehends an alleged maritime criminal could request that criminal's transfer to the receiving country (e.g., Kenya, Seychelles), which would then decide whether to accept the suspect on the basis of an assessment of the available evidence. To augment the arrangements, a special "fast-track" piracy court was opened in Shimo La Tewa, Mombasa, in June 2010. The facility, which was funded with $5 million, most of it from the UN Office of Drugs and Crime, Canada, and Australia, serves as a purpose-built detention center to jail pirates convicted through the Kenyan judicial system. A similar court was opened in the Seychelles in 2011, while a purpose-built prison capable of holding up to 460 inmates was inaugurated in Hargeisa, Somaliland, at the end of March 2011 (GAO, 2010, p. 24; "Kenya Opens Fast Track Piracy Court in Mombasa," 2010; Maliti 2010; UN Secretary-General, 2010, p. 15; "Seychelles to Attend Somaliland Prison Inauguration," 2011).

UN Initiatives

Finally, the United Nations has been instrumental in moving to foster collective action against armed maritime violence around the HoA. In January 2009, the Contact Group on Piracy off the Coast of Somalia was created to serve as an international forum for countries participating in the CP effort in the region.[13] Operating in tandem with CTF-151, the forum has four working parties designed to facilitate and coordinate action in the general areas of information-sharing, judicial capacity-building, situational awareness, diplomatic outreach efforts, and criminal financial tracking (National Security Council, 2008, p. 8; UN, 2009).[14] The group has produced four "best management practice" documents that provide specific advice for vessels operating in the waters off the HoA and how to deter attacks or respond to them when they occur (UK House of Commons Foreign Affairs Committee, 2011, pp. 19–20).[15] As of this writing, ten countries had signed the 2009 New York Declaration (*Commitment to Best Management Practices to Avoid, Deter or Delay Acts of Piracy*), which commits them to promulgating the guidance and ensuring that all vessels on their

---

[13] The group includes representatives from Australia, Austria, the Bahamas, Belgium, Canada, China, Cyprus, the Czech Republic, Denmark, Djibouti, Egypt, Ethiopia, Finland, France, Germany, Greece, India, Indonesia, Italy, Japan, Kenya, the Republic of Korea, Liberia, Lithuania, Malaysia, the Marshall Islands, Mauritius, Mexico, Morocco, the Netherlands, Nigeria, Norway, Oman, Pakistan, Panama, Portugal, Russia, Saudi Arabia, the Seychelles, Singapore, the Somali Government of National Unity, Spain, Sweden, Turkey, Ukraine, the United Arab Emirates, the United Kingdom, and the United States. In addition, it includes observers from the African Union, the EU, NATO, the UN Secretariat, and the International Maritime Organization.

[14] The four working groups are as follows: Working group 1, which is led by the United Kingdom in collaboration with the UN International Maritime Organization, addresses activities related to military and operational coordination, information-sharing, and the creation of a regional coordination center; working group 2, which is led by Denmark, focuses on the judicial aspects of piracy with the support of the UN Office on Drugs and Crime; working group 3, which is led by the United States with the support of the International Maritime Organization, aims to strengthen shipping self-awareness and other capabilities; and working group 4, which is led by Egypt, is devoted to improving diplomatic and public information efforts on all aspects of piracy.

[15] The latest version is *Best Management Practices for Protection Against Somalia Based Piracy*, version 4, August 2011. Advice includes dimming ship lights when traveling near Somali waters; adhering to the designated maritime patrol security area monitored by CTF-151; installing remote-controlled fire hoses, razor wire, and other obstacles to offset vulnerable points of entry; creating a secure "citadel," where a vessel's crew can barricade themselves while still accessing communication equipment and navigational control; maintaining speeds of 18 knots in the event of an attack; and executing heavy wheel turns. Signatories to the New York Declaration include the United States, United Kingdom, Singapore, Panama, the Marshall Islands, Liberia, the Republic of Korea, Japan, Cyprus, and the Bahamas.

respective registries have adopted its provisions (author interviews with International Maritime Bureau personnel, London, May 2009; GAO, 2010, p. 13).

The UN Security Council has also passed several resolutions germane to piracy off the HoA. The most important are UNSCRs 1816, 1846, and 1851, which collectively sanction "cooperating" states to take all necessary measures that are deemed appropriate to suppress Somalia-sourced piracy and armed robbery at sea. UNSCR 1816 and UNSCR 1846 authorize the search and interdiction of suspect vessels in the country's coastal waters, while UNSCR 1851 legitimates actions to disrupt territorial-based dens. The resolutions are unprecedented in the level of authority they grant the international community to counter threats in the maritime realm—extending, in principle, to the use of armed force on land. They are also legally binding on all states ("Action Against Pirate Bases OKd," 2008; Evans, 2008; Leinward, 2008; MacFarquhar, 2008; "UN Maritime Agency Welcomes Security Council Action," 2008; IMB, 2009, pp. 41–42; Wambua, 2009, p. 50).

Assessing International Responses to Piracy off the Horn of Africa
The various measures outlined here have found some success. EU and NATO escort ships have helped ensure the safe delivery of World Food Programme relief supplies and humanitarian aid to Somalia. Given that the number of ships willing to transport food aid to the country had been halved by 2007, this is no small feat (International Maritime Organization and World Food Programme, 2009). Moreover, coalition forces have been instrumental in thwarting several attempted hijackings and, more generally, in securing shipping in the maritime security patrol area. Between 2008 and 2011, incidents in the Gulf of Aden declined by about a third, while the number of successful hijackings perpetrated by Somali gangs declined from 49 in 2010 to 28 in 2011. U.S., international, and industry officials agree that these successes are due, in part, to the international naval presence in the region, as well as the adoption of the best management practices put out by the Contact Group on Piracy off the Coast of Somalia (Gortney, 2009; McDonald, 2009b; Viscusi, 2009; GAO, 2010, p. 64; IMB 2012, p. 24).

No less importantly, the international response represents an unprecedented level of intergovernmental cooperation that has been achieved in a remarkably short period and, frequently, between sovereign entities that have rarely—if ever—operated on a common footing. This collaborative action not only gives concrete expression to the reality that maintenance and regulation of the seas ultimately relies on joint interstate agreement and enforcement, but it also provides the U.S. Navy and partner nations a unique opportunity to engage one another and work out issues of interoperability and coordination. Properly developed, this effort could lay the foundation for an effective regime of maritime order that is able to address piracy and other transnational threats, such as illegal fishing, drug trafficking, and environmental degradation (Chalk, Smallman, and Burger, 2009, p. 4). Such international cooperation is necessary to confront current and future MIW threats facing the United States and its allies, no less so because maritime environments are, by definition, international territories.

That being said, current international CP initiatives fall short, at least with respect to the specific challenge off the HoA. One obvious practical problem concerns the size of the area to be monitored, which (as pirate activity has expanded into the Indian Ocean) now constitutes nearly 2 million square nautical miles and sees more than 33,000 transits a year (GAO, 2010, p. 27; Milmo, 2010).[16] To comprehensively cover this expansive and heavily trafficked maritime space would necessitate a massive naval deployment and far more than the 30 or so ships currently patrolling the region. One U.S. Navy analysis estimated that even basic coverage would require 1,000 ships equipped with helicopters, something that is clearly infeasible (GAO, 2010, p. 29).

Difficulties have become even more attenuated as the locus of attacks has moved to the southern and eastern coasts of Somalia, where patrols are virtually nonexistent, as well as farther down the East African coast toward the Seychelles (McDonald, 2009). These geographic

---

[16] According to the World Shipping Council, more than 7 percent of the global ocean trade, carrying 6.8 billion tons of goods, transited the Suez Canal in 2007. The only alternative route is around the Cape of Good Hope in South Africa, which would add 4,900 nm to a standard journey.

shifts, which have been prompted, at least in part, by the international naval presence in the maritime security patrol area, readily underscore the "balloon effect" associated with attempting to counter a threat that is highly fungible and adaptable in nature (Chalk and Smallman, 2009, p. 40).

A related problem has to do with cost. The direct expenses associated with operating a single frigate at sea are approximately $82,000 per steaming day (GAO, 2010). Using this figure as a base, the total cost of international deployments to the HoA would be approximately $1.3 billion per year (A. Bowden et al., 2010, p. 15). Outlays of this magnitude bring into question the sustainability of the current naval flotilla, especially if there is no discernible decline in attack levels. Moreover, every dollar spent on trying to contain piracy necessarily means that there is less money to invest in other, potentially more viable land-based solutions, which most commentators agree has to be an integral part of any long-term strategy (National Security Council, 2008, p. 5; Greenblatt, 2009, p. 211; author interviews with International Maritime Bureau personnel, London, May 2009; author interview with a Royal Australian Navy officer, Canberra, Australia, May 2009). The cost of deploying one frigate to the Gulf of Aden for six months, for instance, could theoretically cover the wages of 100,000 police officers over the same period; for less than one-fifth of the total amount spent on deployments, a fully equipped and trained Somali coast guard of 1,400 personnel could be made operational (Hansen, 2009, p. 61; Gelfand, 2010).[17] Moreover, it is worth noting that, in addition to operational support costs, the capital costs of a fleet of this size run into the tens of billions of dollars.

The cost dimension of the naval containment strategy takes on further relevance when one considers that it has no dual-use payoff in terms of addressing other threats, such as illegal fishing or environmental degradation. As Stig Jarle Hansen (2009, p. 50) has observed, the current tack could, in fact, exacerbate these challenges: "Interna-

---

[17] In September 2009, a nascent Somali coast guard of 500 recruits was inaugurated. However, the force is completely devoid of assets—it has fewer than a dozen skiffs at its disposal—and is completely reliant on international funds.

tional involvement [off Somalia] might actually promote illegal fishing by decreasing the deterrent effect pirates have on illegal fishers since it scares away the former." This speaks to the point that the MIW commitments that are most costly are more likely to be sustainable if they can be used to address multiple threats simultaneously. Moreover, this example underscores the need to weigh the costs and benefits of land-based versus maritime operations in each IW situation and to make balanced assessments regarding the extent to which each option provides a viable solution both on its own and in combination with other efforts.

The judicial accords also pose difficulties. The main transfer agreement is with Kenya, which forms the centerpiece of these arrangements. However, the court structure in the country is stretched to the limit and lacks efficiency.[18] As of mid-2010, Kenya had prosecuted an estimated 43 pirates but was holding 100 more; of those prosecuted, only 25 have been sentenced to serve prison time. Nairobi has already complained that it is being exploited as a "dumping ground" for captured pirates and, at the end of December 2010, refused to renew the accords after they expired, asserting that, henceforth, it would accept suspects on a case-by-case basis only (UK House of Commons Foreign Affairs Committee, 2011, p. 50). This declaration followed the Kenyan government's threats in early 2010 to pull out of the transfer accords, after which the international community promised to help fund the detention center in Mombasa as a way of cajoling the government to continue its participation. However, this ultimately proved to be a stop-gap solution; the court had only 11 prosecutors—far short of the necessary infrastructure for a fully fledged international tribunal. The same problem will presumably exist with the facility in the Seychelles. With around $4 million being earmarked to support the project, it is doubtful that any more than 40 people could be accommodated in the prison—and even then, only for a maximum of two years each. An additional problem concerns the Seychelles' geographic distance from the HoA and the associated logistical hurdles of transferring suspects in time to satisfy legal requirements that they appear

---

[18] In Kenya, more than 800,000 criminal and civil cases were still pending in 2009 (Houreld and Corder, 2009).

before a judge within 24 hours (GAO, 2010, p. 65; "Kenya Opens Fast-Track Piracy Court in Mombasa," 2010; Maliti, 2010; UN Secretary-General, 2010, p. 16).

The UN Security Council resolutions are likely to give rise to equally difficult challenges, particularly if they are used to sanction military raids and strikes aimed at dismantling pirate dens in Somalia itself. Advocates of this approach argue that such action is legitimated under UNSCR 1851 which, as previously noted, authorizes all participating states to take whatever measures are necessary to deter pirates emanating from Somali maritime and territorial space. Indeed, as of this writing, the EU was actively considering expanding EUNAVFOR's mission to include action aimed at destroying pirate logistical infrastructure on the beach ("EU Mulls Expanding Anti-Piracy Mission to Beaches," 2011). While these types of responses are theoretically permitted, any moves to forcibly disrupt criminal communities on land would likely result in widespread civilian collateral damage, not least because it would be almost impossible to differentiate marauders from ordinary fishermen. At the very least, such responses would cause widespread anti-Western sentiment and could, conceivably, trigger a backlash that serves to dangerously politicize what is presently a nonviolent economic phenomenon (IMB, 2010a, p. 12; IMB, 2010b, p. 11).[19]

Perhaps the most fundamental problem of the current international response, however, is the fact that it is premised solely on a containment strategy. The entire thrust of the measures in place is directed at disrupting piracy at its end point (on the seas), as opposed to addressing it at its root (on land). Again, this speaks to the need to weigh the appropriateness of maritime versus land-based options in every situation, as well as to assess the appropriate operational level of maritime engagement. Whereas MIW capabilities can, in many cases, be employed in a useful manner to modulate U.S. involvement, there are indications that a strategy based solely on containment is not the best

---

[19] Because the main objective of the Somali pirates is to elicit as large a ransom as possible, most gangs avoid harming captives or destroying ships. Indeed, between 2008 and the end of 2011, of the 3,500 seafarers taken hostage, 62 had been killed—less than 2 percent.

option in this case. Frigates and naval deployments pursuing external operations in the region have little, if any, relevance to many of the underlying territorial "push" factors that give rise to armed maritime crime in the first place. In the case of Somalia, these include unemployment, poverty,[20] lack of economic development, and, above all, the absence of sovereign governance. While wholesale nation-building would be an extremely expensive, lengthy, and politically sensitive task,[21] other smaller, targeted, BPC-type MIW initiatives could be usefully applied, such as further fostering the nascent Somali coast guard, providing incentives for coastal communities to desist from providing support to the pirates,[22] and supporting institution-building in the semifunctioning areas of Puntland and Somaliland.[23]

Strategic Scenario 3: Unconventional Warfare in Nicaragua

One of the cases we explored was an example of UW: U.S. support of the Contras in seeking to overthrow the Sandinista government in Nicaragua, particularly the U.S. efforts to mine Nicaraguan ports and harbors in the early 1980s. In this case, the United States employed irregular forces (often through the use of proxy or partner forces) in an attempt to overthrow an existing government. It is worth noting that UW scenarios carry unique politico-strategic challenges. This is illus-

---

[20] Most Somalis live on less than $2 per day.

[21] Certainly, the United States has no appetite for attempting to establish a long-term presence in Somalia following its ignominious retreat from the country in 1993.

[22] For example, protecting local fishing ground and sponsoring small-scale industry and cooperative businesses that do not rely on the piracy financial "lifeline."

[23] Somaliland has already demonstrated an ability to institute a durable and relatively efficient onshore remedy against piracy, while Puntland has elements of governance that exist close to or even in criminal harbors, such as Garad and Eyl. Problematically, however, the international community has largely shunned moves to support these two semiautonomous areas for fear that this will undermine the prospects for a single Somali state. The preference has been to shore up the power of the Government of National Unity in Mogadishu, which presently controls no more than six of the 16 districts in the capital city.

trated by the Nicaragua case, in which overall mission failure was, for the most part, not due to any tactical failing of maritime efforts in UW but, rather, to political miscalculations regarding the country in question. In contrast, the maritime operations in the Nicaragua case were quite successful at the operational and tactical levels. Because UW often involves challenges at the politico-strategic level, and maritime operations can be utilized to decrease both political visibility and the United States' onshore footprint, maritime operations could be used to a greater extent in support of future UW campaigns to strengthen their likelihood of success. Such a policy should be pursued cautiously, however; the Nicaragua case also illustrates that inherent in the unique politico-strategic challenges of UW are risks to U.S. standing in global public opinion. Recall that IW, by definition, involves a population with whom the adversary and friendly coalition are trying to gain legitimacy and influence. The U.S. partner may only have to influence and monitor the sensibilities of a *local* population, but this case shows that the legitimacy of U.S. involvement in MIW operations—both UW and otherwise—may be tested in *worldwide* public opinion. Because the United States is a leading global power, its stakes may be higher, and it may have more to lose than does its partner, even though the partner may face most of the operational dangers.

While the lessons of the Nicaragua case are useful, it is also a unique case. For instance, the U.S. partner (the Contras) became aware of the mining operations only after the fact, and contractors hired by the U.S. Central Intelligence Agency (CIA), rather than U.S. military or partner forces, conducted the operations. One should therefore exercise caution in generalizing from this case study to other cases of maritime UW. We nonetheless consider this an example of UW because the United States was engaged in a broader UW mission to support the Contras during this period, and the maritime operations were a component of this broader strategy aimed specifically at establishing the conditions for the U.S. partner to succeed. Other cases of UW operations in the maritime realm might lead to different findings, however. Analysis of such cases would therefore pose a fruitful avenue for future research.

Background: U.S. Policy in Nicaragua

The United States has a long history of intervening in Nicaraguan affairs, dating back to the 19th century. By 1927, the United States had 11 warships in Nicaraguan ports and nearly 5,400 marines in Nicaraguan cities (Booth, 1985, p. 40). Just as the last detachment left the country in 1933, the U.S. government used its influence to help Anastasio Somoza Garcia become the first commander of the Nicaraguan National Guard. Somoza forcefully took control of the government in 1936, ruling with his sons until 1979. During this time, the United States depended on Nicaragua for unequivocal support of its Cold War activities in the Caribbean: Nicaragua provided military bases for the CIA's efforts to overthrow a left-wing government in Guatemala in 1954, it supported the Bay of Pigs invasion in 1961, and it provided troops to assist the U.S. military intervention in the Dominican Republic in 1965 (Brennan, 1999; Tierney, 2006).

However, the Somoza regime weakened when President Jimmy Carter suspended all military and economic assistance to Nicaragua in 1977 in response to Somoza's record of human rights abuses. The assassination of journalist Pedro Joaquin Chamorro and the takeover of the National Palace by Eden Pastora and 25 Sandinistas in 1978 further weakened Somoza's influence (Brennan, 1999; Tierney, 2006). The Sandinista National Liberation Front then led a successful popular uprising on July 19, 1979, overthrowing Somoza and instituting plans for a revolutionary Nicaragua. Suddenly, the leadership of Nicaragua was connected to Cuba and the Soviet Union politically, philosophically, and militarily.

Meanwhile, the Reagan administration made clear that it would not tolerate "another Cuba" in the western hemisphere. The administration therefore opted to provide covert assistance to an emerging "counter-revolution" as a proxy for direct U.S. military involvement. This decision to use covert force was made following a Pentagon estimate that a full-scale U.S. intervention in Nicaragua would require 125,000 troops over a period of four to six weeks to defeat the Sandinistas and could result in more than 4,000 U.S. casualties (Brennan, 1999, p. 7). The administration chose to use political and economic sanctions, in conjunction with the covert support of a counter-revolution and periodic threats of military escalation, in an effort to alter the foreign policy of Nicaragua and, ultimately, to force the Sandinistas from power (Brennan, 1999, p. 9). According to Sylvan and Majeski (2009),

> In late 1981, President Reagan approved an 11-point program for "Cuba and Central America," the key point of which was to carry out political and paramilitary operations "against the Cuban presence and Cuban-Sandinista support infrastructure in Nicaragua and elsewhere in Central America." An accompanying CIA "scope" paper specified that this would involve "the formation and training of action teams" which would be "primarily" non-U.S. in nature; the aim of these teams' paramilitary activities would, in the words of a formal presidential "finding," be "to facilitate" a new regime in Nicaragua. (Sylvan and Majeski, 2009, supplemental materials)

President Reagan signed the top-secret National Security Decision Directive 17 on January 4, 1982, giving the CIA the authority to recruit and support the Contras with $19 million in military aid (Reagan, 1982).

U.S. Mining of Nicaraguan Harbors
One component of the broader U.S. strategy to overthrow the Sandinistas during this period consisted of the CIA-planned mining of Nicaraguan ports and harbors in the hopes of discouraging oil shipments, strangling the Nicaraguan economy, and undermining the military efforts of the official Sandinista government (Clarridge, 1997, pp. 262–265; Brennan, 1999, p. 274). A top-secret memorandum written by National Security Council staff members Oliver North and Constantine Menges noted that the "intention [of the mining was] to severely disrupt the flow of shipping essential to Nicaraguan trade during the peak export period" (North and Menges, 1984; Richelson, 2002, p. 228; Brennan, 1999, p. 275). The goal was also to "further impair the already critical fuel capacity in Nicaragua." In one particular case, according to North and Menges,

while we could probably find a way to overtly stop the tanker from loading/departing, it is our judgment that destroying the vessel and its cargo will be far more effective in accomplishing our overall goal of applying stringent economic pressure. It is entirely likely that once a ship has been sunk no insurers will cover ships calling in Nicaraguan ports. (quoted in Richelson, 2002, p. 228)

The operations utilized irregular tactics, personnel, and equipment. South American contract employees working for the CIA—so-called "unilaterally controlled Latin assets"—carried out the mining and other maritime operations in support of the Contras using modified gunboats known as "Q-boats." These Q-boats were civilian cigarette-type speedboats that the U.S. Customs Service had confiscated from drug traffickers. The CIA strengthened the boats' structures and mounted a 25-mm chain gun on each boat's bow and a 40-mm automatic grenade launcher on each stern, which made them able to effectively destroy any coastal target in Nicaragua.

Beginning in October 1983, Q-boats attacked oil and gas storage tanks in the port of Corinto. All the tanks exploded, along with a crane needed to load and unload cargo at the port, closing the port until replacement parts could be located and shipped from the Netherlands. As a result of this attack, more than 3 million gallons of fuel burned out of control for most of the day, causing the evacuation of 25,000 residents of the port city (Meislin, 1983). Then, in January and February 1984, Q-boats were used to deploy more than 70 Mark 36 sea mines at Corinto, Puerto Sandino, Puerto Cabezas, and El Bluff at the mouth of the Bluefields Harbor on the Atlantic coast (Gutman, 1988, p. 197; Brennan, 1999, p. 274). Because these "firecracker" mines were not being produced for any Western military arsenal, the CIA had them made to its own design specifications at a workshop near Honduras (Gutman, 1988, p. 197).

The Nicaraguan Democratic Force (FDN), one of the earliest Contra groups, took credit for the mining. Edgar Chamorro Coronel, the leader of the FDN, issued a report that his forces "have the capacity to sink any Mexican oil tanker delivering crude at Puerto Sandino." In a radio broadcast, rebel spokesman Adolfo Carrero Portocarrero said,

"The anchoring zone and the port itself has been mined, and therefore the Nicaraguan Democratic Force is not responsible from now on for the safety of any ships operating in those waters" ("Nicaraguan Guerrillas Report Laying Mines at a Key Port," 1983). Yet, as Edgar Chamorro Coronel later reported in an affidavit,

> On January 5, 1984, at 2am, the CIA deputy station chief of Tegucigalpa, the agent I knew as "George," woke me up at my house in Tegucigalpa and handed me a press release in excellent Spanish. I was surprised to read that we—the FDN—were taking credit for having mined several Nicaraguan harbors. "George" told me to rush to our clandestine radio station and read this announcement before the Sandinistas broke the news. The truth is that we played no role in the mining of the harbors. But we did as instructed and broadcast the communiqué about the mining of the harbors. Ironically, approximately two months later, after a Soviet ship struck one of the mines, the same agent instructed us to deny that one of "our" mines had damaged the ship to avoid an international incident. (Chamorro, 1985, pp. 18–19)

Thus, the Contras were not aware of the mining when it was conducted. Yet, given the context in which the mining operations occurred, as well as the stated U.S. goals of the mining, it is clear that these operations were a component of the larger U.S. strategy to support the Contras, aiming to establish the conditions whereby the Contras could succeed in overthrowing the Sandinista government.

The mining achieved its short-term tactical aims, damaging or sinking numerous international ships. Two small fishing boats off the Caribbean port of El Bluff were the first to hit the mines and sank on February 25, 1984 (Gutman, 1988, pp. 198–199). A Dutch dredger was seriously damaged at Corinto on the Pacific coast on March 1, 1984, and a Panamanian freighter also detonated a mine in early March. A Soviet tanker reported damage at Puerto Sandino on the Pacific coast on March 20, 1984 (leading to a Soviet protest note), and Liberian, Panamanian, and Japanese ships also triggered explosions (Gutman, 1988, p. 199). All in all, six Nicaraguan vessels and six ships from five other nations were damaged, though none was confirmed sunk, and ten sailors were seriously injured ("Explosion Over Nicaragua," 1984). At least eight merchant marine vessels turned back from Nicaraguan ports to find safer waters, including a Mexican oil tanker carrying 75,000 barrels of much-needed fuel. All in all, the mining operation cost the Nicaraguans more than $10 million: Cotton and coffee piled up on the docks, and imports and exports had to be trucked to and from ports in neighboring Central American countries (Richelson, 2002, p. 228).

Despite this tactical success, however, the mining's broader strategic aims were not achieved, and the effort had unintended political consequences that affected the larger UW mission and U.S. funding for the Contras. The Reagan administration expected that shipping to Nicaragua would be halted for 30 or so days and that this would cause a "big ripple" of news. But, according to a senior State Department official at the time, "No one cared. International shippers ignored it. It didn't affect one shipping line's schedule. Insurance companies were blasé about it" (Gutman, 1988, p. 198). Meanwhile, news of U.S. involvement in the mining led both houses of Congress to schedule hearings into the Nicaraguan situation in April 1984, and seven House members introduced a resolution demanding an immediate end to the mining of Nicaraguan harbors ("Democrats Rip Policy on Mining Nicaragua Ports," 1984). The ultimate outcome of the mining was a Senate vote of 84-12 against the use of U.S. funds to "plan, direct, execute, or support the mining of the territorial waters of Nicaragua." This was a nonbinding resolution but a strong rebuke of the CIA, revealing bipartisan opposition (Gutman, 1988, pp. 200, 202–203).[24]

Revelations of U.S. involvement in the mining operation also earned the United States international condemnation and, hence, decreased U.S. legitimacy in global public opinion. France offered to sweep the mines if "one or several friendly European powers" were willing to cooperate (Gutman, 1988, p. 201). Then, on March 30, 1984, the Sandinistas introduced a resolution in the UN Security Council denouncing the United States for "the escalation of acts of military

---

[24] Notably, however, Reagan administration officials continued to aid the Contras through foreign donations and covert, private weapon sales.

aggression brought against" Nicaragua. France and the Netherlands voted in favor, Britain abstained, and the United States had to cast a veto ("Explosion Over Nicaragua," 1984). On April 9, 1984, Nicaragua asked the International Court of Justice to find the mining and U.S. support of the Contras a violation of international law.[25] All in all, while this case illustrates that MIW can enable limited military commitments, it also illustrates that strategic success is—at least at times— contingent upon more than the tactical and operational success of maritime forces and that the United States may face higher stakes than its partners in winning public support for its MIW activities.

Each of the cases examined in this chapter profiles MIW from the standpoint of the United States or its allies. To put forth a more complete understanding of MIW from the viewpoint of U.S. adversaries or actors resembling them, the next chapter explores three cases of MIW with a focus on enemy capabilities and tactics.

---

[25] The United States, however, told the World Court in advance that it would not recognize the court's jurisdiction over Central American matters for two years. State Department spokesman John Hughes explained that Washington felt that it could not get a fair hearing because, among other reasons, it could not defend itself adequately against Nicaragua's charges without disclosing secret intelligence information. A U.S. government statement added, "We do not wish to see the court abused as a forum for furthering a propaganda campaign" ("Explosion Over Nicaragua," 1984).

CHAPTER FIVE

Adversary Capabilities in Maritime Irregular Warfare

The future is uncertain regarding the range of potential MIW threats that may face the United States. Yet, it is informative to examine the breadth of capabilities possessed by U.S. adversaries or analogous actors in the recent past and at present. This chapter aims to identify and assess the spectrum of possible future MIW threats that the United States may confront. To this end, we explored the cases of the Sea Tigers (the maritime wing of the LTTE), active in Sri Lanka from 1984 through 2009; the LeT attack in Mumbai in 2008; and piracy off the HoA over the past decade. Notably, in our examination of piracy in this chapter, we focus specifically on pirate capabilities (as opposed to the CP initiatives explored in Chapter Four). While not all are adversaries of the United States specifically, the three groups examined in this chapter are illustrative of the enemies that the United States confronts in the IW arena. They can therefore inform an analysis of the threats that the United States and its allies could potentially confront in the future. Taken together, these three cases paint a picture of current and potential future MIW adversaries that possess a vast range of technical capabilities and are often well organized, quite adept at ISR, and employ successful recruitment tactics.

LTTE Sea Tigers, 1984–2009

The LTTE was originally founded as the Tamil New Tigers in 1972. Led by Chetti Thanabalasingham, the Tamil New Tigers embarked on a particularly intensive campaign of assassination and violence that was

variously designed to silence progovernment Tamils, eliminate infor-
mants, and disrupt police investigations into terrorist incidents and
related criminal activities perpetrated in the group's name. In 1976, the
group suffered a major blow when Thanabalasingham was arrested. His
second-in-command, Velupillai Prabhakaran, subsequently assumed
leadership, renaming the group the LTTE. Affirming the legitimacy of
the Tamil struggle for independence on the basis of the Thimpu principles (Ponnambalam, 1998),[1] and specifying that the Tigers' ideological
objectives could be achieved only through violence, Prabhakaran fash-
ioned a uniquely elite and ruthlessly efficient fighting force that emphasized selective recruitment and an unswerving dedication to the Eelam
cause (Gunaratna, 1987; Wijesekera, 1993; Samaranayake, 1999).

Over the course of the intervening 30 years, the Tigers gained
a reputation as one of the most sophisticated and deadly terrorist
insurgencies in the world. The group demonstrated a proven ability
to operate along a full combat spectrum, including selective assassina-
tions through acts of urban sabotage, civilian-directed bombings, hit-
and-run attacks, and full-scale frontal assaults. More importantly, the
LTTE was able to take and hold large tracts of territory across northeast Sri Lanka, as well as resist and then decisively respond to concerted
offensives instituted by the Sri Lankan Armed Forces. It was this combination of resilience and effectiveness that essentially drove Colombo
to accept terms for a so-called cease-fire agreement in 2002. Brokered
by Norway on February 22, the accord opened the way for several
rounds of talks during which the LTTE was given de facto control of
an autonomous area in northeast Sri Lanka, complete with its own tax
structure, judiciary, police, and health and educational structure (IISS,
2004; "Peace Process Bogged Down," 2004; "Peace Talks," 2004;
Smith, 2005; author interviews in Bangkok, Thailand, and Colombo,
Sri Lanka, May 2004 and April 2005).

---

[1] The Thimpu principles affirmed the following four nonnegotiable demands: (1) recognition of Tamils as a nation, (2) recognition of the existence of an identified homeland for the
Tamil people, (3) recognition of the right of the Tamil people to self-determination, and
(4) recognition of the right of the Tamil people to a separate citizenship.

Although the cease-fire agreement did raise hopes that a final peace settlement could be achieved with the LTTE, repeated violations of the accord and fears that the group was exploiting the cessation of active combat to build up its own forces eventually led to the collapse of the agreement in 2006. Large-scale hostilities quickly resumed, which saw some of the bloodiest fighting of the more than three-decade war. By May 2009, the LTTE had been reduced to a small sliver of land in the northeast, where it made its last stand. Banning reporters from the region and reportedly ignoring the safety of Tamil civilians, the Sri Lankan Army launched an all-out offensive against this rump force. During the offensive, the army captured or killed all remaining LTTE combatants, including Prabhakaran, who reportedly died while making a final charge against troops in an armor-plated van filled with armed rebels (Blakely, 2009; Magnier, 2009; McDonald, 2009a; McDonald and Cowell, 2009; Mydans, 2009).

Overview of Operations and Enemy Capabilities

During its existence as an active militant entity, the LTTE engaged in an extensive array of irregular maritime activities that embraced both attack and logistical modalities. From the very beginning, the LTTE recognized that a maritime arm to the organization was essential. The group's supreme leader, Prabhakaran, made this clear when he remarked, "Geographically the security of Tamil Eelam is interlinked with that of the seas. [It is] only when we are strong in the seas and break the dominance our enemy now has that we will be able to retain the land areas we liberated and drive our enemies from our homeland" (quoted in Hariharan, 2006). It was to this end that the LTTE created a dedicated maritime wing in 1984. Falling under the control of Thillaiyampalam Sivanesan (aka Colonel Soosai) and known as Kadal Puli, or Sea Tigers, the unit played a pivotal role in the Tigers' overall order of battle until the eventual defeat of the insurgency in May 2009 (Murphy, 2009, p. 311). The Sea Tigers therefore exemplify what the United States might expect from its most capable MIW adversaries in the near term.

At their height, the Sea Tigers had a combined strength of between 2,000 and 3,000 cadres.[2] These personnel were split between functional departments covering engineering, maintenance, communications, underwater demolition, and naval training and operations (conventional and nonconventional). The main bases of the wing spanned the eastern coastline of Sri Lanka, running from Chundikulam in the north to areas near to Trincomalee in the south (Suryanarayan, 2003; Rahman, 2004, p. 8; Ramachandran, 2006; Murphy, 2009, p. 312).[3]

The primary role of the Sea Tigers was to reduce the mobility of the Sri Lankan Navy around the northeastern coast (Sakhuja, 2005; Bogollagama, 2007; Murphy, 2009).[4] Marine operations, though nominally independent of the territorially based component of the LTTE, were specifically designed to support the Tiger ground offensive in two respects: first, to secure coastal entry points for the importation of weaponry procured overseas, and second, to cut government maritime resupply routes to military units deployed on the Jaffna Peninsula (the Tigers' geographic focus and the symbolic heart of the aspirational Eelam state). Attacks were directed against a range of Sri Lankan naval assets, including offshore patrol vessels, submarine chasers, Dvora/ Super Dvora fast assault ships, personnel carriers, and amphibious landing craft (Balachandran, 2006).

---

[2]   It is estimated that at least half of these cadres were killed in the tsunami that struck Sri Lanka in 2004.

[3]   During the cease-fire agreement, the LTTE demanded de facto "sovereign" status for the Sea Tigers and full rights over all contiguous offshore resources. Had this demand been conceded (the Norwegian-led mediation team did briefly broach the idea of an exclusive economic area for the group), it would have given the Tigers control over two-thirds of Sri Lanka's coast, effectively establishing a third navy in the region. This would have had direct implications for both Sri Lanka and India, and, as such, the idea was never countenanced.

[4]   Besides marine warfare, the Sea Tigers were also linked to opportunistic acts of piracy against commercial carriers that strayed too close to their operational waters. Between 1990 and 2001, attacks occurred at the rate of about two per year, after which they became less frequent (arguably a by-product of the cease-fire agreement and the perceived need to project the image of an organization engaged in a completely bona fide struggle for national liberation). In most instances, container ships would be temporarily boarded with the aim of stealing cargoes that could be used to support the war effort. However, there were also claims that the LTTE hijacked entire vessels, reflagging them in open-registry countries to build up the ranks of the Sea Pigeons, the LTTE's main maritime logistical arm.

The Sea Tigers benefited from both innovative tactics and innovative uses of fairly standard maritime technologies. They typically operated in squadrons of three boats each, with attacks mounted at night to avoid aerial counterstrikes.[5] Assaults generally employed Tiger "wolf packs" that singled out and surrounded Sri Lankan Navy surface combat, patrol, and utility ships. These packs would then either fire on their targets or ram them with suicide boats. In the former case, the Sea Tigers used tactical craft equipped with 23-mm twin-barrel cannons, backed up by four 12.7-mm machine guns and various combinations of rocket launchers. In the latter case, specially modified "cigar" torpedo riders would be employed. These secondary vessels were typically constructed out of fiberglass (to maximize speed and maneuverability), designed to lie low in the water, powered by 250-horsepower outboard engines, and typically rigged with ten to 14 claymore mines connected in a circuit to three booster charges. Certain vessels were also equipped with bow-mounted compressible steel rods that were connected back to onboard explosive packs. Intended primarily as self-detonation devices, they had the ancillary benefit of amplifying the force (and destructive power) of resultant shockwaves by puncturing the hulls of targeted ships *before* detonation occurred ("LTTE Suicide Kit," 2001; Balachandran, 2006; Murphy, 2009, p. 313).

While the Sea Tigers engaged in both conventional and irregular maritime warfare, suicide strikes arguably constituted the signature trait of their operations. Attacks were mostly carried out by teams of two or three volunteers and were specifically designed to induce a chronic state of tactical and strategic paralysis in the enemy.[6] In excess of 40 martyr missions were executed between 1990 and 2008, over 80 percent of which were deemed to have been instrumental in achieving their primary aim (author interviews in Colombo, Sri Lanka, May 2004). According to one retired senior naval officer, the fear of

---

[5] The Sri Lankan air force had only a rudimentary night-vision capability and hence tended to engage the Sea Tigers only during daylight hours.

[6] This is different from the suicide attacks executed on land, which were carried out by a highly trained, elite subunit of the LTTE (the Black Tigers) that remained at the pinnacle of the group during its operational existence.

being caught in a suicide attack was one of the main factors contributing to a decrease in recruitment in the Sri Lankan Navy during the 1990s. This psychological effect had considerable strategic significance because it allowed the LTTE to maintain effective control over expansive stretches of Sri Lanka's northeastern coastline for many years (author interviews, Colombo, Sri Lanka, 1999).

The tactical significance of Sea Tiger suicide attacks was no less marked. Indeed, the group was conducting assaults similar to that undertaken against the USS *Cole* and MV *Limburg* as far back as 1990. This suggests not only that the LTTE was eight to ten years ahead of al Qaeda in terms of seaborne capabilities, but also that, more intrinsically, it defined the critical benchmark guiding developments in the wider area of MIW (author interviews in Colombo, Sri Lanka, May 2004).

One aspect that undoubtedly contributed to the Sea Tigers' effectiveness was the emphasis placed on investing in and honing surface and underwater combat capabilities. To defeat Sri Lankan naval radar scans, for instance, attack vessels were deliberately designed with angled metallic superstructures that reduced their signature cross-section. Sea Tiger teams would also typically sail in close formation, hugging the coastline. The technique was designed to mask the electronic trail of individual craft by avoiding sonar signals altogether or, failing this, giving the impression of one large vessel. The tactic was based on the same procedure used by combat air wings to avoid aerial surveillance and, according to Sri Lankan intelligence officials, was highly effective in facilitating covert approaches and surprise strikes against naval frigates, destroyers, and transporters (author interviews in Bangkok, Thailand, April 2005).

In addition to its use of surface vessels, the LTTE invested a great deal of time and effort in refining underwater strike modalities and munitions. The group successfully manufactured mines that could be put together using cheap and readily available household items, such as rice cookers. At least two variants of submersible improvised explosive devices were developed: rapid-detonation explosive slabs that could be attached to the hull of a target ship using a black glycerol mixture and cylindrical bombs (roughly 60–90 centimeters in height) that could be suspended from a vessel's rudder or propeller shaft. Both devices were equipped with delayed-timer switches (author interviews, Singapore, April 2005; Murphy, 2009, p. 9).

The Sea Tigers are now known to have built mini-submarines to covertly debus martyrs in strategically and commercially significant harbors, such as Colombo and Trincomalee.[7] Revelations that the LTTE was making concerted moves in this direction first broke in 2000, when a partially completed prototype was discovered at a Tamil-owned shipyard in Phuket. According to informed sources, the five-meter vessel, while rudimentary, was capable of remaining submersed for up to six hours (at speeds of approximately five knots) and could very well have served as the blueprint for the more advanced versions that the Sea Tigers subsequently retained ("Lanka Suspects Submarine in Thailand to be LTTE's," 2000; Davis, 2000, p. 28; author interviews, Colombo, Sri Lanka, May 2004).[8]

Finally, the LTTE effectively supplemented its own research and development efforts by illegally procuring advanced combat weaponry from sovereign state sources. Sri Lankan intelligence officials have evidence of at least two major arms purchases that the LTTE concluded with China's North Industries Corporation (Norinco) in 2003. The deals, which reportedly included consignments of ammunition, assault rifles, and light artillery large enough to fill a 70-meter cargo ship, were arranged through a middleman as part of a wider order secured with fraudulent North Korean end-user certificates (Rosenberg, 2007). Further indications of potentially illicit Asian sales surfaced in 2007, when the Sri Lankan Navy captured a locally modified "giant boat" off Point Pedro on the Jaffna Pensinsula. The vessel was equipped with a Chinese-manufactured 14.5-mm twin-barreled canon and Japanese-built outboard motors and radar systems that, in the words of government officials, could not normally be obtained without "proper per-

---

[7] Sri Lankan sources also believe that the move to develop submarines was driven by the navy's purchase of new-generation Israeli-built Dvora fast-attack craft at the end of the 1990s, which were proving effective against the Sea Tigers' surface ships.

[8] There have been claims that the LTTE attempted to purchase underwater attack and transport vessels from North Korea, although these allegations have never been proven.

mission from a government" (Jayasiri, 2007a, 2007b; Murphy, 2009, p. 319).

Insights to Inform Future Maritime Irregular Warfare

Given the tactical and technological innovativeness of the Sea Tigers, their willingness to perpetrate suicide attacks, and their ability to obtain materials and weaponry from international sources, the group sets a high threshold for the level of capability that future MIW adversaries of the United States and its allies might possess. The case therefore embodies several warnings for U.S. forces that might engage in MIW, particularly in a CT role. First, before beginning operations, it is essential to have a competent and current estimate of the adversary's capabilities. Second, U.S. and partner forces should be aware that their adversaries can adapt and become much more lethally capable if they are given sufficient time to do so.

While other MIW adversaries may not necessarily possess the high level of technological capability and inventiveness seen in the case of the Sea Tigers, other, more low-tech qualities—such as the ability to organize and recruit members and to conduct successful reconnaissance and surveillance missions—are just as important to consider when scoping future U.S. MIW capabilities.

Lashkar-e-Taiba Attack in Mumbai, 2008

For a 60-hour period from November 26 to 29, 2008, a small team of gunmen from the Pakistani LeT jihadist group attacked the Indian port city of Mumbai, which also happens to be the country's main business, cultural, and tourist center. They spread chaos throughout the city by striking at major hotels, the main railway station, a café, and a Jewish community center. By the time all the terrorists had been either killed or captured, 172 Indian civilians, police, and soldiers had been killed and the confidence of the Indian public in its government security forces had been shaken (Binnie and La Miere, 2009). One of the most intriguing aspects of this attack, from the perspective of military analysts, is that it began with an approach from the Arabian

Sea. This makes it one of the more ambitious maritime terrorist attacks launched so far by the international jihadist movement.

LeT, which had thus far concentrated most of its attacks in India's Kashmir province, apparently had a number of objectives in mind for the 2008 Mumbai operation.[9] Perhaps most importantly, the group wished to increase tensions between India and Pakistan to force the Pakistani government to move large numbers of its army units away from the western tribal regions (where they were battling various jihadist groups friendly to LeT) and into areas along the Indian border. Such a redeployment would reduce the pressure on the jihadist forces operating in the Federally Administered Tribal Areas (FATA) of Pakistan. Secondary objectives for the attack included embarrassing the Indian government in front of the world media and its own people, stoking Hindu-Muslim tensions in India, and terrorizing U.S., British, and Israeli tourists and expatriates in Mumbai.

The 2008 Mumbai attacks differed from previous jihadist spectaculars in some important ways. As noted earlier, the LeT used a maritime approach to strike a major urban target. However, the attack did not involve the detonation of massive explosive charges, and it was not a dedicated suicide operation. Finally, the employment of small teams of lightly armed gunmen to sequentially attack a wide range of symbolic targets was something not seen before from the international jihadist movement.

Overall, the LeT maritime attacks in Mumbai have to be rated as a partial strategic success. The operation did not cause an outright Indo-Pakistani conflict, nor did it force a halt to Pakistani army operations in FATA. It did, however, dominate the international media headlines for three days and make the Indian government look weak and ineffective. Furthermore, the Mumbai operation created a new "heroic narrative" for jihadists around the world—one in which a tiny band of lightly armed jihadists was able to hold one of the largest cities in the non-Muslim world hostage for almost three days until finally being overwhelmed by the superior numbers and firepower of the Indian

---

[9] The South Asian Terrorism Portal website includes a discussion of LeT's history, objectives, and ideology. See "Lashkar-e-Toiba: 'Army of the Pure,'" undated.

Army and police. Thus, there is concern among several governments in Europe and elsewhere that these attacks will serve as a blueprint for similar assaults in the future.

Overview of Operations and Enemy Capabilities

The Mumbai operation involved meticulous preattack planning by the LeT. The ten terrorists who executed the attack studied satellite images of Mumbai for months before they departed from Pakistan; they also reviewed blueprints of the two major hotels they were going to attack (Rabasa et al., 2009, p. 3). Various reports indicate that the LeT pre-positioned weapons and ammunition at certain secret locations in Mumbai.

Approximately five days prior to the attack, the ten operatives left Karachi on a Pakistani cargo ship. While in the Indian Ocean, they hijacked an Indian fishing trawler and used that vessel to transit to Mumbai's coastal waters (Rabasa et al., 2009, pp. 3–4). Once there, they killed the Indian trawler captain and his crew and transferred to two inflatable dinghies on the night of November 26. In the darkness, they landed at two debarkation points in South Mumbai, escaping detection by the Indian authorities. The LeT terrorists were armed only with standard assault rifles and grenades, along with a few very crude improvised explosive devices.

One two-man team moved to Mumbai's huge Chhatrapati Shivaji Terminus train station and opened fire on the crowds of evening commuters (Rabasa et al., 2009, p. 5). Another two-man team attacked the Nariman House Jewish community center and took 13 hostages. A third two-man team struck the elegant Trident-Oberoi Hotel, rampaging through the property and killing guests at random. Finally, a single four-man team struck the Taj Mahal Palace Hotel and the nearby Leopold Café.

After the initial strikes were over, the team at the train station moved on to attack the Cama and Albless Hospital before hijacking a police car. At that point, they were finally intercepted and killed by police. The Nariman House team murdered five hostages before being overrun a day later by Indian Army commandos. The Trident-Oberoi Hotel team held out in that building for 17 hours before being killed.

Finally, the Taj Mahal Palace Hotel team held out the longest, fighting for 60 hours before being killed by Indian commandos. Eventually, nine of the terrorists were killed and one was captured.

The attack's success was due to well-executed standard raiding tactics. The teams used a covert maritime infiltration to the target: their use of a hijacked Indian trawler made it all but impossible for the poorly funded Indian Coast Guard to intercept them at sea. Once ashore, the attack teams used maximum surprise and rapid movement to paralyze the local police. The attack teams were dispersed and used urban clutter as cover. Simultaneous strikes were launched to create the impression among the media and Mumbai authorities that a much larger force was involved. Furthermore, there is some evidence to suggest that LeT operatives had sufficient intelligence to avoid the most capable police units in Mumbai during the first attacks.

The major innovation on the part of the terrorists was likely the real-time exploitation of the international media. Each of the terrorists carried a BlackBerry smartphone to monitor CNN and BBC Internet coverage of the attack in real time (Rabasa et al., 2009, p. 7). They then immediately adjusted their tactics to increase the amount of media coverage that the attacks would receive. It is believed that the major efforts made by the terrorists to kill U.S. and British civilians were part of the plan to garner more international press coverage.

However, the early tactical successes achieved by the LeT teams were not solely due to the skill of the terrorists; the Indian response to the attacks was very flawed and thus aided the terrorists greatly. Indian intelligence provided no concrete warning to the authorities in Mumbai in the days before November 26, so officials were completely stunned when the assault began. Poor coastal surveillance by the Indian Coast Guard made it easy for the terrorists to come ashore unnoticed. Perhaps worst of all was the poor performance of the local Mumbai street police (McElroy, 2008; Sahni, 2008). With low levels of training and few good weapons, the local police were completely paralyzed by the initial attacks. Once the operation was fully under way, it took 12 hours before India's elite Army CT commando unit (the Black Cats) arrived in Mumbai by air from its base near New Delhi. Apparently, the unit was not able to quickly obtain an airlift that could fly it to Mumbai. Once on the ground in Mumbai, the commandos' counterattack planning process was slowed because they lacked good blueprints of the two major hotels being attacked.

Insights to Inform Future MIW

This case illustrates both the advantages and disadvantages that can accrue to a terrorist enemy from a maritime approach to a target. In terms of advantages, a maritime approach can allow operatives to avoid border crossings and airport security, and, if the terrorists have access to fast boats for ingress and egress, they can spend only a minimal amount of time in the target city. Transit across the open ocean may offer plenty of opportunities to quietly hijack a local vessel to allow the attackers to blend in with the normal local coastal traffic. Additionally, maritime transit may offer terrorist teams some extra time for preattack planning, as well as extra time for rest just before the attack commences. Finally, a maritime insertion can allow terrorists to select very precise landing sites and infiltration routes.

However, the Mumbai operation also demonstrated the shortcomings inherent in a maritime terrorist attack approach. First of all, once a full blown, large-scale urban assault has started, it may be very difficult to exfiltrate the operatives. Second, the transport of large explosives aboard crude fishing vessels and trawlers is risky; thus, maritime terrorist strikes may have to rely on small arms to do their damage. There are obviously limits to what can be done with assault rifles and grenades, even when complete surprise is achieved. Third, as the Mumbai episode showed, some kind of reconnaissance cell would likely have to be sent to the target city well in advance of the attack; this could create opportunities for a skilled intelligence service to place surveillance teams on the reconnaissance cell and ultimately to break up the plot before the assault team can even embark. While this problem could also be associated with urban attacks initiated from land, it is relevant to note that it remains a problem in attacks with a maritime approach. Finally, a maritime approach does not allow the terrorist team to fully disperse until it lands ashore. Even if the operatives approach in two or three different small boats, the interception of just one of the boats could drastically reduce the team's numbers and effectiveness.

There are a number of concrete measures that the United States and its allies can take to reduce the chances of a recurrence of this type of attack. Probably most importantly, policymakers around the globe might consider funding and maintaining large, high-quality coast guards to defend against such threats. If the Indians had had a robust coast guard working in the Arabian Sea, the LeT may have been deterred from even attempting the Mumbai operation. Coast guard vessels can be supplemented with civilian coast watch volunteers in remote areas. Also, the international community could consider placing automated hijack alert systems on larger fishing vessels and trawlers (similar to panic buttons in U.S. banks), which would allow the crews of large and medium-sized fishing vessels to quickly broadcast encrypted hijack distress signals to regional navies and coast guards.

At the source of the problem, intelligence agencies should consider increasing their surveillance of maritime training programs at jihadist camps in Pakistan, Yemen, and (especially) Somalia. These agencies should also work to prevent pirates and jihadists from joining forces in the HoA. It would be very threatening to all maritime nations if the jihadists were able to acquire many of the tactics, techniques, and procedures used by Somali pirates over the past several years in the Gulf of Aden. Finally, it would be sensible to fund expanded port security measures in ports that are likely jihadist points of embarkation, such as Karachi, Aden, and Mogadishu.

Piracy off the Horn of Africa

The waters of the HoA—an area that encompasses the territorial seas of Somalia, the Gulf of Aden, and the southern Red Sea—currently constitute the most pirate-prone region of the world, and piracy in this region has been on the rise in recent years. Between 2008 and 2011, a total of 776 actual or attempted acts of piracy occurred in this strategic corridor, accounting for just under 50 percent (48.8 percent) of all global incidents during the period (IMB, 2010a, p. 5; IMB, 2010b, p. 5). While the concentration of piracy remains greatest near Somali shores, attacks now cover a vast area of the Indian Ocean that stretches as far south as Mozambique and as far east as the Maldives (Nincic, 2009, p. 5; Straziuso, 2009; Wambua, 2009, p. 49; IMB, 2012, p. 20).

Capabilities of Perpetrating Groups

Groups operating off the HoA vary in size and complexity, ranging from small subsistence entities with one or two personnel and a skiff to larger organizations of several dozen personnel equipped with a wide array of maritime craft. Gangs generally revolve around a respected leader (usually a veteran pirate), and most members come from a fishing background and are linked by common clan, blood, or tribal allegiances (Hansen, 2009, p. 39).[10] Typically, these personnel will be split into attack, hold, and reconnaissance teams (Program for Total Conflict Leadership, 2006; Hansen, 2009, p. 36; Schiemsky, 2009, pp. 40–43). As a rule, the attack teams garner the most respect and receive the lion's share of any negotiated ransom. The first to board a ship is especially favored and bestowed with considerable social prestige. In the words of one gang member, "When you capture a ship people welcome you like a president" (Hansen, 2009, p. 40). Costs are usually borne by the leader (who also takes most of the ransom), shared among the members, or met by outside investors. In all three cases, however, the pirate commander will be connected in his community and thus able to draw upon an extensive personal network for protection and problem solving (Hansen, 2009, pp. 25, 34–35).

Historically, the Hoboyo-Harardhere cartel (sometimes referred to as the Somali marines or Somali coast guard) and syndicates based in Puntland have dominated much of the piracy scene in Somalia. The former entity was largely the product of one man, Mohamed Abdi Hassan "Afweyne" (a former civil servant) and mainly operated 400 kilometers north of Mogadishu out of Ceel-Huur and Ceel-Gaan. By the end of 2006, the group was thought to have a militia of between 75 and 100 and a flotilla of at least 100 skiffs (Schiemsky, 2009, pp. 40–43). Farah Hirsi Kulan (aka "Boyah," considered the "father" of piracy in Puntland) was key to the latter, acting as the principal

---

[10] It should be noted that, in certain cases, Somali gangs recruit across lineage lines to ensure that they attract the best and most experienced personnel available.

recruiter, organizer, and financier for missions of several hundred pirates operating out of the Eyl area (Backhaus, 2010). Although still major players, these syndicates now compete with a diffuse mosaic of groups based in several coastal hamlets down the 1,888-mile Somali coastline. Current main hubs include Eyl, Garard, and Ras Asir,[11] and between 1,500 and 3,000 pirates are thought to be active off Somalia overall (UK House of Commons Foreign Affairs Committee, 2011, p. 13).

Syndicates are well armed and have access to a wide assortment of combat weaponry, including assault rifles, heavy and light machine guns, and RPGs. Most of these arms are procured from illegal bazaars in Somalia, Ethiopia, and Sudan, where munitions are both plentiful and relatively cheap. According to a self-confessed Mogadishu-based trader, one alleged pirate transaction in May 2008 included ten AK-47s and 140 boxes of ammunition; eight PK machine guns and 190 boxes of ammunition; four RPGs and 60 rounds; two DShK heavy machine guns and 200 boxes of ammunition; and 60 hand grenades (Schiemsky, 2009, pp. 45).

Although equipped with an array of weaponry, Somali pirates are generally low-tech, illustrating that the range of technological capabilities among these MIW actors and others, such as the LTTE Sea Tigers, for example, is wide. Contrary to popular wisdom, the use of night-vision goggles, GPS, satellite phones, and ship identification units is rare (Hansen, 2009, p. 36). By contrast, most gangs simply pick targets according to their size and calculated vulnerability, as evidenced by the characteristic low free board (the distance from the upper deck to the waterline), slow speed (generally less than 15 knots), absence of onboard defensive measures (such as barbed wire and fire hoses), and medium to large tonnage (which are presumed to elicit higher ransom demands) of targeted ships (author interview with a Royal Australian Navy officer, Canberra, Australia, July 2009; GAO, 2010, p. 8). The gangs' ability to calculate these vulnerabilities speaks to a fairly well-

---

[11] Bosaso is also home to pirate gangs but does not act as an operational base per se. Kismayo used to be a prominent den, but syndicates have mostly been driven out since the Islamist group al Shabab took control of the city a few years ago.

refined system of tacit knowledge among their personnel regarding the characteristics of vessels that are susceptible to attack, as well as good surveillance and reconnaissance practices.

Despite this low level of technological capability, the pirates' tactical capability appears to be fairly high. While most incidents currently occur close to Somali shores (largely due to the displacement effect of maritime patrols in the Gulf of Aden), gangs have exhibited an ability to act extremely far out to sea. Pirates, operating from "mother ships," have been reported as far east as the Maldives and as far south as the Mozambique Channel and tend to migrate as weather conditions around the HoA deteriorate (GAO, 2010, p. 27; UK House of Commons Foreign Affairs Committee, 2011, p. 14). One particularly well-publicized attack was the 2008 hijacking of the Saudi-registered MV *Sirius Star*, which occurred more than 500 nm from Somalia (Otterman and McDonald, 2008; Worth, 2008). Other long-distance incidents have included the MV *Maersk Alabama* (250 nm from the town of Eyl), the USS *Nicholas* (west of the Seychelles), and the USS *Ashland* (330 nm from Djibouti) (GAO, 2010, p. 16).[12]

Unlike in other pirate-infested waters in Southeast Asia, the vast majority of attacks off the HoA (more than 93 percent) occur during daylight hours, indicating a certain level of confidence among the pirates regarding their ability to execute their tactics successfully, despite international efforts in the region to identify and arrest them. Each attack lasts, on average, between 30 and 45 minutes. Incidents also closely mirror seasonal weather conditions, following the transition between the northeastern and southwestern monsoon periods (Combined Maritime Forces, 2009; author interviews with maritime security specialists, Copenhagen, Denmark, March 2010).

Once on board, pirates will generally round up the crew and detain them below deck. Depending on the size of the hijacked vessel, they will either force the captain and his first officer to pilot it back to Somali waters or they will sail it themselves. The ship will then be

---

[12] The *Nicholas* and *Ashland* incidents were not attempted hijackings; rather, they involved "defensive" fire after the U.S.-flagged vessels approached the pirates' positions (presumably for the purposes of interdiction).

docked at a port under the control of the attacking gang, where it will remain until negotiations for its release are finalized. While anchored, fuel to power generators and supplies such as food and water are rendered from vendors on shore (author interview with a Royal Australian Navy officer, Canberra, Australia, July 2009; author interviews with maritime security specialists, Copenhagen, Denmark, March 2010).[13]

Insights to Inform Future MIW

Although it does not pose a major strategic threat to any one state, piracy off the HoA does illustrate that future MIW adversaries may pose economic rather than military threats. Furthermore, the case illustrates that these financial costs might be imposed with relatively minimal investments backing the operations themselves. The actual financial cost accrued by the pirates will vary by operation, but a basic, opportunistic hijacking probably amounts to no more than $500, assuming that the gang already owns its boats. The more expensive (though still relatively resonable) cost is the maintenance of the ship after it has been seized, which can add up to as much as $100 per day (Hansen, 2009, p. 38).[14] In the case of smaller hijackings, costs are either fronted by the pirate leader or collectively borne by the gang's members. For operations involving the seizure of large oceangoing freighters, outside investors usually provide the necessary funds. Since payments are made in cash and then transferred through the unofficial *hawala* remittance system,[15] the money trail has proved exceptionally difficult to follow. Nevertheless, law-enforcement officials believe that the financial backing for piracy in this region principally comes from mafia bosses based in Somalia, Lebanon, Dubai, and Europe (author interviews with maritime security specialists, Copenhagen, Denmark, March 2010).

---

[13] In this way, piracy has served to stimulate local cottage industries along the Somali coast, and, in many cases, communities in prominent dens such as Eyl and Garard have little motivation to see the practice eradicated, because it is viewed as an economic lifeline.

[14] Assuming a 40-day negotiation process, maintaining a hijacked vessel could therefore cost the pirates as much as $4,000.

[15] Payments are usually made in denominations of U.S. $50 bills (largely because the $100 note is so widely forged) and airdropped close to the hijacked vessel.

These investments can result in large payoffs. Payments for the release of ships have steadily increased as larger freighters have been seized. Whereas settlements in the late 1990s and early 2000s would be in the hundreds of thousands of dollars, today, sums are in the millions. In 2011, Somali gangs netted an estimated $135 million ("Somali Pirates Obtained Over USD 135 Million Ransoms in 2011," 2011). To date, the largest single payout has been $10 million, made in November 2010 to secure the release of the South Korean supertanker *Samho Dream* ("Piracy at Sea," 2011).

Interestingly, however, because the essential aim is to elicit as large a payment as possible, violence is typically not a feature of piracy off the HoA (unlike the situation in West Africa and Southeast Asia). In most cases, hostages are treated relatively well and reports of forced starvation and abuse appear unfounded (Gettleman, 2009a). This was certainly the opinion of Colin Freeman, the chief correspondent for the UK's *Daily Telegraph* newspaper, who was kidnapped along with his photographer in November 2008 and held for six weeks. Both were treated well and fed goat's meat during their time in captivity. According to Freeman, this reflects the general practices of Somali pirates who have mostly "been at pains to treat their hostages well, knowing that a businesslike approach makes it all the more tempting for the ship owners to resolve things by ransom than by force" (Freeman, 2009). Indeed, between 2008 and the end of 2011, of the 3,500 seafarers taken hostage, only 62 were killed—less than 2 percent (UK House of Commons Foreign Affairs Committee, 2011, p. 17).

The case of piracy off the HoA therefore illustrates the opposite end of the spectrum of future MIW adversaries relative to the case of the LTTE Sea Tigers. Unlike the Sea Tigers, pirates in this region tend to utilize fairly traditional technologies and focus more on financial gain than on inflicting casualties or achieving any sort of military success. While they certainly do not have weak ISR abilities—as demonstrated by their ability to identify ships vulnerable to hijackings— neither do the pirates have the highly technical ISR capabilities of the Sea Tigers. Like the Sea Tigers, however, the pirates are capable recruiters and have a number of personnel at their disposal.

CHAPTER SIX

Conclusions and Recommendations

Given the current prominence of irregular warfare and related activities in U.S. military strategy, it is reasonable to explore the various advantages of IW activities on land, in the air, and in maritime environments. Yet, there is a dearth of analysis on the specific requirements of and opportunities provided by maritime IW at present, with very little focus in the doctrinal and other literature on IW in maritime environs. The aim of our study was to describe the strategic potential of MIW and to assess its operational and tactical characteristics based on a sample of recent MIW operations, with an eye toward informing future U.S. force structure investments and future doctrine regarding the maritime aspects of IW. The analysis in the previous chapters includes several key findings and points that are relevant to the design of future U.S. military policy regarding MIW missions, on which we elaborate, in turn, in the following section. This chapter then concludes with a series of recommendations to enhance future U.S. MIW operations.

Key Findings

A Definition of Maritime Irregular Warfare
We find that MIW comprises, at various times, both irregular and conventional warfare activities, perpetrated by both irregular and conventional forces, against irregular and conventional enemies. The combination of actors and methods involved determines whether the activity in question qualifies as MIW, in our view. To do so, at least one

actor must be irregular, and the operations must take place in a maritime environment, including riverine operations. In its consideration of both the actors and tactics involved, our conception of MIW goes beyond earlier actor-focused doctrinal definitions of IW.

Furthermore, our case-study analyses of MIW reflect the applicability of existing IW doctrine to MIW, particularly in the characterization of IW as often involving a state (such as the United States) providing some form of assistance to a partner (either a host-nation or nonstate force), which allows for the possibility of indirect lines of operation on the part of the United States (or other intervening state). MIW, like IW as defined in doctrine, also typically involves a population with which both the adversary and friendly coalition are trying to gain legitimacy and influence.

For the purposes of this study, we thus defined MIW as operations involving at least one irregular actor or tactic that aim to shape the maritime environment in at least one of three ways: (1) to prevent supplies or personnel support from reaching an adversary, (2) to increase the capacity of partner naval and maritime forces, or (3) to project tailored U.S. power ashore to directly confront adversary forces, when necessary.

The OEF-P Case Compared to Other Historical Cases of Maritime Irregular Warfare: Lessons Learned

The study's main findings span the strategic, operational, and tactical levels. Several are specific to MIW, while others have implications for both MIW specifically and for IW operations more broadly.

First, as was seen in the OEF-P case, much IW takes place on land and is conducted by ground forces. Maritime force therefore often plays a largely supportive role to land-based IW operations, even in maritime environments such as the Philippine archipelago. *Because maritime force is generally considered to play a supportive role to ground forces in IW, it has the potential to be underutilized even in IW operations conducted in a predominantly maritime environment.* This is illustrated by the early years of OEF-P, when maritime force was used only sparingly in the largely maritime archipelago environment of the Philippines. Therefore, policymakers and military planners should weigh the costs and benefits of land-based versus maritime operations in each IW situation and make balanced assessments regarding the extent to which each option provides a viable solution both on its own and in combination with other options. On a related note, from a tactical planning perspective, maritime forces sometimes conduct IW operations in nontraditional environments (such as on land) and perform nontraditional functions (such as leading Provincial Reconstruction Teams and building schools). This has occurred in Colombia, in Iraq during OIF, and in OEF in Afghanistan. Conversely, U.S. Army and other ground-based forces sometimes conduct maritime operations in IW campaigns, as was seen in Vietnam. Moreover, the Vietnam case illustrates that riverine MIW can benefit from a combined-arms approach, so it is sensible to consider how maritime and ground-based forces can be used in tandem to conduct MIW operations.

Second, as seen in OEF-P, *countries that have a prevalent maritime dimension associated with an insurgency could potentially benefit from the enhancement of CMOs in the maritime arena.* CMOs in OEF-P have tended to be land-based. However, given that the aim of such operations is to win support among the population for COIN efforts, the population's focus in the OEF-P case on earning a livelihood in the maritime environment points to the potential for maritime-focused CMO approaches in this and similar environments. Furthermore, the Vietnam experience shows that in riverine COIN, just as in land-based COIN, strike operations against main insurgent units should be followed up by efforts to enhance local public support if final victory is to be achieved. Such operations provide one potential mechanism for enhancing public support; they might, for instance, aim to revitalize ports and harbors in areas that are largely economically dependent on fishing, as was done in OEF-P.

Third, *maritime operations in IW can allow the United States to scale its ground involvement in useful ways.* Because MIW capabilities often allow U.S. forces to operate with relatively high mobility, low visibility, and a small footprint, maritime forces offer a military option when host-nation sensitivities or U.S. preferences constrain the deployment of U.S. ground forces. For example, sea-based forces in the Sulu Archipelago are more mobile, responsive, and capable of supporting

AFP missions across larger coastal areas of the archipelago than are land-based special forces teams.

Fourth, if one assumes that future MIW engagements that entail building a partner's capacity will resemble OEF-P, *it is important to manage strategic expectations based on realistic assessments of the partner's capabilities.* By properly scaling U.S. efforts in a way that kept the AFP successful but also kept the AFP in the lead, OEF-P's IW campaign has encouraged development and promoted the AFP's legitimacy among the Filipino population. The personnel limits and other constraints placed on U.S. forces in OEF-P are argued to be one reason that the AFP is investing more in its navy and developing practical new capabilities for the Sulu Archipelago, such as the Coast Watch South coastal surveillance system paired with additional combatant craft. Yet, scaling U.S. activities and strategic expectations in this manner can be challenging, particularly when U.S. forces must limit their own activities and sacrifice short-term effectiveness for long-term partner viability.

Fifth, *the OEF-P case indicates that, when building partner capacity either in MIW or land-based IW, the United States should make efforts to provide equipment and technology that the partner will be able to maintain and operate without difficulty.* Because of the Philippines' minimal military-industrial infrastructure and its navy's small training budget, U.S. forces need to pass along equipment and teach tactics that are low-tech, low-cost, practical, reliable, and easy to maintain. Sustainable equipment and training for the partner in this case consists of small combatant craft, outboard motors, very high-frequency and high-frequency radios, nautical charts, compasses, surface radars, small arms, and basic seamanship tools, all of which the Philippine Navy would reasonably be able to repair and could afford to maintain. Again, this might pose a challenge for U.S. forces trained and practiced in operating more high-tech equipment. Another equipment-related problem in the context of BPC has been evident in the United States' gifting of old or obsolete equipment to the Philippine Navy, which creates problems in accessing spare parts. In many cases, the Philippine Navy has managed to build its own spare parts, but it is worthwhile to note that this is a potential challenge facing partnering nations that have unequal technical capabilities and types of equipment (author interviews with Philippine Navy personnel, January 2009).

Sixth, *with regard to operational methods, coastal maritime interdiction can play an instrumental role in setting the conditions for success in IW by cutting the supply lines that sustain an insurgency.* Previous research on COIN has shown that the presence or absence of sanctuary for the insurgents is a very important variable determining success of the COIN force (Gompert and Gordon, 2008). As such, maritime approaches can become an important domain of IW as insurgents work to keep open and exploit sea lines of communication and counterinsurgents seek to disrupt these lines and use them to support their own mobility and logistics. This was demonstrated in various maritime operations in the Vietnam War and has been successfully employed in Colombia as well. Coastal and riverine interdiction may also be easier to conduct than ground interdiction when enough ISR assets and naval platforms are devoted to the task on a constant basis. However, a comparison of the cases of Vietnam and OEF-P demonstrates that geography plays a major role in determining the level of ease with which such interdiction operations may be conducted. In the context of an archipelago resembling the Philippines, maritime interdiction may be vastly more challenging than along coastlines resembling that of Vietnam.

Seventh, as the Nicaragua case illustrates, *U.S. partners in MIW may only have to influence and monitor the sensibilities of a local population, but the legitimacy of U.S. involvement may be tested in worldwide public opinion.* The stakes for the United States—as a global power— may be higher, and it may have more to lose than its partners, even though U.S. partners may face most of the operational dangers. While the Nicaragua case is so unique that it may not be generalizable to other cases of UW in maritime environs, this particular lesson applies to any MIW activities that the United States or other global powers may conduct.

Finally, *international cooperation in confronting MIW adversaries is often necessary, and the U.S. Navy should make an effort to ensure that it is tactically and operationally interoperable with partner navies in order to facilitate coordination.* This is illustrated by the case of counterpiracy off the HoA, but it is more widely applicable due to the international nature of the maritime environment.

The Range of Capabilities of U.S. MIW Adversaries

This monograph assesses three recent or ongoing cases of MIW from the standpoint of U.S. adversaries. The Colombian case explored in Chapter Four provides some insight into the issue of potential future threats, as do three cases explored in Chapter Five: the Sea Tigers wing of the LTTE in Sri Lanka (1984–2009), the 2008 LeT terrorist attack in Mumbai, and the ongoing threat posed by pirates operating off the HoA. In examining these cases, we sought to derive lessons regarding the range of capabilities that future U.S. MIW adversaries could possess. What emerges from these case analyses is an image of MIW adversaries with a wide spectrum of technical capabilities that are often well organized, quite adept at ISR, and employ successful recruitment tactics.

For example, an adaptive and technically proficient irregular enemy can challenge maritime forces in IW. Before beginning operations, it is therefore essential for U.S. forces to have a competent and current estimate of the adversary's capabilities. U.S. and partner forces should be aware that their adversaries can adapt and become much more lethally capable if they are given sufficient time to do so. The challenges posed by adaptive, technically proficient irregular enemies is seen in the case of narcotics traffickers in Colombia, in which the traffickers switched from moving large shipments of cocaine in single consignments on fishing trawlers to using go-fast boats to smuggle smaller amounts of cocaine in stages. This change was initiated following several major drug seizures between 2002 and 2006. The traffickers' heightened use of semi- and fully submersible vessels to smuggle drugs out of the country is another example; this practice has increased with the growth of U.S. and Colombian Navy capabilities to catch traffickers' go-fast boats. Another example of a highly capable, technically proficient MIW adversary is the LTTE Sea Tigers, who benefited from both innovative tactics and innovative uses of fairly standard maritime technologies.

Yet, even when they do not enjoy high-tech advantages, MIW adversaries can pose substantial and challenging threats. At the other end of the spectrum of MIW adversary capabilities from the LTTE Sea Tigers, Somali pirates are generally equipped with an array of low-tech weaponry. Despite this relatively low level of technological prowess, pirate gangs have exhibited an ability to act extremely far out to sea and have displayed a system of tacit knowledge among their personnel regarding the characteristics of vessels that are susceptible to attack, in addition to good surveillance and reconnaissance practices. Moreover, future MIW adversaries may pose economic rather than strategic or military threats. This is also seen in the case of piracy off the HoA, which demonstrates that these financial costs can often be imposed with relatively minimal investments backing the operations themselves.

A third lesson derived from these cases is that terrorist enemies may enjoy several advantages from a maritime approach to a target. The case of the LeT attacks in Mumbai illustrates some of these advantages. A maritime approach allows operatives to avoid border crossings and airport security, can offer opportunities to quietly hijack a local vessel so that the attackers can blend in with local coastal traffic, and offers terrorist teams some extra time for preattack planning as well as extra time for rest just before the attack commences. Finally, a maritime insertion allows terrorists to select very precise landing sites and infiltration routes.

However, terrorist enemies may also face several disadvantages from a maritime approach to a target, some of which were seen in the LeT attacks in Mumbai. First, once a full blown, large-scale urban assault has started, it may be very difficult to exfiltrate the operatives. Second, the transport of large explosives aboard crude fishing vessels and trawlers can be risky; thus, maritime terrorist strikes are limited to relying on small arms to do their damage. Third, some kind of reconnaissance cell will likely have to be sent to the target city well in advance of the attack, creating opportunities for a skilled intelligence service to place surveillance teams on the reconnaissance cell and break up the plot before the assault team can commence. Finally, a maritime approach does not allow the terrorist team to fully disperse until it lands ashore. Even if the operatives approach in two or three different small boats, the interception of just one of the boats would drastically reduce the team's numbers and effectiveness.

Recommendations

The findings presented here have several direct implications for the future U.S. conventional Navy and NSW. First, our examination of various MIW cases from both the friendly and enemy perspectives, taken together, make clear that coastal powers possess inherent vulnerabilities that enemies may exploit and that such exploitation could lead to the targeting of commercial ports and shipping. This implies that the United States could benefit from maintaining operational and tactical capabilities with which to assist its partners in surveillance, particularly against small submarines and mining threats. It further indicates that U.S. naval forces should continue to develop capabilities to provide U.S. partners with suitable equipment that they will be able to operate and maintain and that they should continually strive to increase their interoperability with partner forces. U.S. naval forces may also have to continue or expand training of partner forces to confront future MIW threats, particularly in developing and executing concepts of operations for maritime sovereignty.

When conducting MIW, operating from a sea base offers advantages to NSW. MIW campaigns can be lengthy, and both the conventional Navy and NSW should be prepared to support sea basing of assets for extended periods. NSW forces, being lighter and thus more adaptable than the conventional Navy, should be able to sustain ship-based operations almost indefinitely. However, due to the costs of such a practice, both NSW and the conventional Navy must also recognize that decisions regarding when and where to support sea basing of this sort must be made carefully.

In support of future MIW operations, NSW will have ongoing requirements for maritime interdiction and containment. Our study indicates that in conducting these campaigns, NSW should consider that future MIW adversaries may be well organized and adept at ISR. It should also consider increasing its capacity to conduct maritime-based CMOs. Doing so would involve increasing SEAL and SWCC (naval special warfare) language and cultural awareness capabilities. Alternatively, NSW and joint force planners could consider teaming up SEALs and SWCCs with Army CMO specialists to conduct maritime CMOs.

Conventional U.S. naval forces should similarly consider their role in supporting significant irregular ground operations launched from the sea, as well as their role in interdiction and containment campaigns. As opposed to naval special warfare, conventional U.S. Navy capabilities to support IW might entail CMOs and related activities to a greater extent than direct action.

In addition to these recommendations, which are specific to NSW and conventional U.S. naval forces, this monograph makes several broader policy-relevant recommendations pertaining to MIW. First, to prevent and deter against maritime attack approaches such as that seen in the Mumbai case, policymakers around the globe might consider funding and maintaining large, high-quality coast guards. U.S. partner coast guard vessels can be supplemented by the use of local civilian coast watch volunteers in remote host-nation areas.

Second, to counter the threat of piracy, the international community might consider placing automated hijack alert systems on larger fishing vessels and trawlers (similar to panic buttons in U.S. banks) that would allow the crews of large and medium-sized fishing vessels to quickly broadcast encrypted hijack distress signals to regional navies and coast guards.

Third, to prevent and deter MIW attacks in a broad sense, intelligence agencies should consider increasing their surveillance of maritime training programs at jihadist camps in Pakistan, Yemen, and (especially) Somalia. These agencies should also work to prevent pirates and jihadists from joining forces in the HoA region. Many maritime nations would be threatened if jihadists were able to acquire many of the tactics, techniques, and procedures used by Somali pirates over the past several years in the Gulf of Aden.

Finally, to deter and prevent MIW attacks more broadly, it would be sensible to fund expanded measures to prevent jihadists from embarking on attack operations from certain high-threat ports, such as Karachi, Aden, and Mogadishu.

References

Abuza, Zachary, *Militant Islam in Southeast Asia: Crucible of Terror*, Boulder, Colo.: Lynne Rienner Publishers, 2003.

"Achieving Security in the Southern Philippines," *Strategic Comments*, Vol. 13, No. 1, February 2007.

"Action Against Pirate Bases OKd," *New York Times*, December 17, 2008.

Allen, Thad, "Guest Post: Transnational Threats Require Transnational Solutions," *SOUTHCOM Commander's Blog*, November 29, 2008. As of October 13, 2011: http://www2.southcom.mil/AppsSC/Blog.php?id=27

Alsema, Adriaan, "US to Invest at Least US$511 Million in Plan Colombia in 2010," *Colombia Reports*, August 26, 2009. As of August 24, 2011: http://colombiareports.com/colombia-news/news/5590-us-to-invest-at-least-us511-million-in-plan-colombia-in-2010.html

Andrade, Dale, *Ashes to Ashes: The Phoenix Program and the Vietnam War*, Lexington, Mass.: Lexington Books, 1990.

Backhaus, Kerin, "Piracy in the Puntland Region of Somalia," *OilPrice.com*, May 12, 2010. As of August 24, 2011: http://oilprice.com/Geo-Politics/Africa/Piracy-In-The-Puntland-Region-of-Somalia.html

Bakshian, Douglas, "Philippine Marines on Front Line in War on Terror," Voice of America, February 20, 2007. As of August 24, 2011: http://www.voanews.com/english/archive/2007-02/2007-02-20-voa16.cfm?moddate=2007-02-20

Balachandran, P. K., "Lanka Most Militarized in South Asia: Study," *Hindustan Times* (India), September 21, 2006. As of August 24, 2011: http://www.strategicforesight.com/sfgnews_186.htm

Bandel, Carolyn, and Kevin Crowley, "Somali Pirate Attacks Sink Premiums as Insurers Leap Aboard," Bloomberg, August 2, 2008.

Bassett, William B., *The Birth of Modern Riverine Warfare: U.S. Riverine Operations in the Vietnam War*, Newport, R.I.: U.S. Naval War College, February 13, 2006.

Best Management Practices for Protection Against Somalia Based Piracy, version 4, Edinburgh, Scotland: Witherby Publishing Group, August 2011. As of August 24, 2011:
http://www.shipping.nato.int/SiteCollectionDocuments/BMP4_web.pdf

Binnie, Jeremy, and Christian La Miere, "In the Line of Fire: Could Mumbai Happen Again?" *Jane's Intelligence Review*, January 2009.

Blakely, Rhys, "Tamil Deaths Mount in Camp," *Weekend Australian*, July 11–12, 2009.

Bogollagama, Rohitha, "Sri Lanka's Perspective on Maritime Security in the Region and Its Relevance to the World," *Asia Tribune*, June 4, 2007.

Boot, Max, "Pirates, Then and Now," *Foreign Affairs*, July–August 2009.

Boot, Max, and Richard Bennett, "Treading Softly in the Philippines," *Weekly Standard*, January 5–12, 2009, pp. 22–28.

Booth, John, *The End and the Beginning: The Nicaraguan Revolution*, 2nd ed., Boulder, Colo.: Westview Press, 1985.

Bowden, Anna, Kaija Hurlburt, Eamon Aloyo, Charles Marts, and Andrew Lee, *The Economic Cost of Maritime Piracy*, working paper, Broomfield, Colo.: One Earth Future Foundation, December 2010.

Bowden, Mark, "Jihadists in Paradise," *Atlantic Magazine*, March 2007. As of August 24, 2011:
http://www.theatlantic.com/magazine/archive/2007/03/jihadists-in-paradise/5613/

Brennan, Richard R., Jr., *The Concept of "Type C" Coercive Diplomacy: U.S. Policy Towards Nicaragua During the Reagan Administration, 1981–1988*, dissertation, University of California, Los Angeles, 1999.

Briscoe, C. H., "Balikatan Exercise Spearheaded ARSOF Operations in the Philippines," *Special Warfare*, Vol. 17, No. 1, September 2004, pp. 16–25.

Button, Robert W., Irv Blickstein, Laurence Smallman, David Newton, Michele A. Poole, and Michael Nixon, *Small Ships in Theater Security Cooperation*, Santa Monica, Calif.: RAND Corporation, MG-698-NAVY, 2008. As of August 24, 2011:
http://www.rand.org/pubs/monographs/MG698.html

Cala, Andres, "Spain Arraigns Somalis Suspected of Piracy," *New York Times*, October 14, 2009.

Chalk, Peter, *The Maritime Dimension of International Security: Terrorism, Piracy, and Challenges for the United States*, Santa Monica, Calif.: RAND Corporation, MG-697-AF, 2008. As of August 24, 2011:
http://www.rand.org/pubs/monographs/MG697.html

Chalk, Peter, and Laurence Smallman, "On Dry Land: The Onshore Drivers of Piracy," *Jane's Intelligence Review*, August 2009.

Chalk, Peter, Laurence Smallman, and Nicholas Burger, *Countering Piracy in the Modern Era: Notes from a RAND Workshop to Discuss the Best Approaches for Dealing with Piracy in the 21st Century*, Santa Monica, Calif.: RAND Corporation, CF-269-OSD, 2009. As of August 24, 2011:
http://www.rand.org/pubs/conf_proceedings/CF269.html

Chamorro, Edgar, *Case Concerning Military and Paramilitary Activities in and Against Nicaragua (Nicaragua v. United States of America)*, affidavit, September 5, 1985.

"China to Send Fresh Anti-Piracy Navy Convoy: State Media," Agence France Presse, October 29, 2009.

Clark, William J., Christopher S. Kelley, and Justin M. Bummara, *Analysis of Maritime Support Vessels and Acquisition Methods Utilized to Support Maritime Irregular Warfare*, Monterey, Calif.: Naval Postgraduate School, June 2010.

Clarridge, Duane R., *A Spy for All Seasons: My Life in the CIA*, New York: Scribner, 1997.

"Cocaine Submarine Seized July 2," *National Geographic Daily News*, July 13, 2010. As of August 24, 2011:
http://news.nationalgeographic.com/news/2010/07/photogalleries/100713-cocaine-submarines-subs-smuggling-drugs-world-crime-pictures/

Combined Maritime Forces, "Combined Task Force (CTF) 151," homepage, undated. As of August 24, 2011:
http://www.cusnc.navy.mil/cmf/151

———, "Shared Awareness and Deconfliction (Shade) Meeting," briefing, April 2009.

Contact Group on Piracy off the Coast of Somalia, "Third Plenary Meeting of the Contact Group on Piracy off the Coast of Somalia," May 29, 2009. As of August 24, 2011:
http://www.state.gov/r/pa/prs/ps/2009/05/124106.htm

Corder, Mike, "Nations Look to Kenya as Venue for Piracy Trials," *Seattle Times*, April 17, 2009.

Council of the European Union, "Current Total Strength of EU-NAVFOR Atalanta," undated. As of August 24, 2011:
http://www.consilium.europa.eu/uedocs/cmsUpload/naviresfinaout.pdf

Cummins, Chip, "U.S. to Lead New Anti-Piracy Force," *Wall Street Journal*, January 8, 2009.

Davis, Anthony, "Tracking Tigers in Phuket," *Asiaweek*, Vol. 29, No. 23, June 16, 2000. As of August 24, 2011:
http://www.cnn.com/ASIANOW/asiaweek/magazine/2000/0616/nat.security.html

Demick, Barbara, "China May Fight Piracy off Somalia," *New York Times*, December 18, 2008.

"Democrats Rip Policy on Mining Nicaragua Ports," *Milwaukee Sentinel*, April 10, 1984.

DoD—*see* U.S. Department of Defense.

"EU Mulls Expanding Anti-Piracy Mission to Beaches: Germany," Associated Press, December 31, 2011.

"European Union to Deploy Anti-Piracy Operations Planes in the Seychelles," African Press Agency, August 30, 2009.

Evans, Michael, "American Commandos Get UN Go-Ahead to Hunt Down Somali Pirates," *The Times* (London), December 18, 2008. As of August 24, 2011:
http://www.timesonline.co.uk/tol/news/world/africa/article5361682.ece

"Explosion Over Nicaragua," *Time*, April 23, 1984. As of August 24, 2011:
http://www.time.com/time/magazine/article/0,9171,921667,00.html

FAS—*see* Federation of American Scientists.

Federation of American Scientists, "Abu Sayyaf Group (ASG)," last updated May 4, 2006. As of August 24, 2011:
http://www.fas.org/irp/world/para/asg.htm

"Fighting One Half of the Drug War: Colombia," Washington, D.C.: Center for Public Integrity, 2009. As of August 24, 2011:
http://projects.publicintegrity.org/report.aspx?aid=255

Freeman, Colin, "Why Somali Piracy Is Booming—By Former Hostage Victim," *Daily Telegraph* (UK), April 11, 2009. As of August 24, 2011:
http://www.telegraph.co.uk/news/worldnews/africaandindianocean/somalia/
5142032/Why-Somali-piracy-is-booming---by-former-hostage-victim.html

Fridovich, David P., and Fred T. Krawchuk, "Winning in the Pacific: The Special Operations Forces Indirect Approach," *Joint Force Quarterly*, Vol. 44, First Quarter, 2007, pp. 24–27.

Fulton, William B., *Vietnam Studies: Riverine Operations, 1966–1969*, Washington, D.C.: U.S. Department of the Army, 1985.

GAO—*see* U.S. Government Accountability Office.

Gelfand, Lauren, "Somalia Agrees to Establish Coastguard to Battle Piracy Threat," *Jane's Defence Weekly*, June 2010.

Gettleman, Jeffery, "Somalia's Pirates Flourish in a Lawless Nation," *New York Times*, October 31, 2008.

———, "Somali Pirates Seize Up to Five More Ships," *New York Times*, April 7, 2009a.

———, "The West Turns to Kenya as Piracy Criminal Court," *New York Times*, April 24, 2009b.

Gilmore, Gerry J., "Kenyan Government Agrees to Try Pirates Seized by U.S. Forces," American Forces Press Service, January 29, 2009.

Gilpin, Raymond, *Counting the Costs of Somali Piracy*, working paper, Washington, D.C.: United States Institute of Peace, July 2009. As of August 24, 2011:
http://www.usip.org/publications/counting-the-costs-somali-piracy

GlobalSecurity.org, "Rigid-Hull Inflatable Boat," web page, last updated July 7, 2011a. As of August 24, 2011:
http://www.globalsecurity.org/military/systems/ship/rhib.htm

———, "Philippine Navy Organization," web page, last updated July 9, 2011b. As of August 24, 2011:
http://www.globalsecurity.org/military/world/phillipines/navy-org.htm

Gompert, David C., and John Gordon IV, *War by Other Means: Building Complete and Balanced Capabilities for Counterinsurgency, RAND Counterinsurgency Study—Final Report*, Santa Monica, Calif.: RAND Corporation, MG-595/2-OSD, 2008. As of August 24, 2011:
http://www.rand.org/pubs/monographs/MG595z2.html

Gortney, William, "DoD News Briefing with Vice Adm. Gortney from the Pentagon," transcript, Washington, D.C.: U.S. Department of Defense, January 15, 2009. As of August 24, 2011:
http://www.defense.gov/transcripts/transcript.aspx?transcriptid=4341

Greenblatt, Alan, "Attacking Piracy: Can the Growing Global Threat Be Stopped," *CQ Global Researcher,* Vol. 3, No. 8, August 2009.

Guerrero, Rustico O., *Philippine Terrorism and Insurgency: What to Do About the Abu Sayyaf Group*, Quantico, Va.: Defense Technical Information Center, 2002.

Gunaratna, Rohan, *War and Peace in Sri Lanka*, Colombo: Institute of Fundamental Studies, 1987.

Gustin, Sam, "U.S. Marines Recapture Ship Held by Somali Pirates," *DailyFinance.com*, November 9, 2010. As of August 24, 2011:
http://www.dailyfinance.com/
story/u-s-marine-commandos-recapture-ship-held-by-somali-pirates/19626852/

Gutman, Roy, *Banana Diplomacy: The Making of American Policy in Nicaragua, 1981–1987*, New York: Simon and Schuster, 1988.

Hansen, Stig Jarle, *Piracy in the Greater Gulf of Aden: Myths, Misconceptions and Remedies*, Oslo: Norwegian Institute for Urban and Regional Research, 2009.

Hanson, Stephanie, *Combating Maritime Piracy*, Washington, D.C.: Council on Foreign Relations, January 7, 2010. As of August 24, 2011:
http://www.cfr.org/publication/18376/combating-maritime-piracy.htm

Hariharan, R., *Sri Lanka: How Strong Are the Tigers?* Nodia, India: South Asia Analysis Group, Note No. 297, February 28, 2006. As of August 24, 2011:
http://www.southasiaanalysis.org/%5Cnotes3%5Cnote297.html

Harwood, Matthew, "Drug War's Rough Waters," *Security Management*, June 2009. As of August 24, 2011:
http://www.securitymanagement.com/article/drug-wars-rough-waters-005658?
page=0%2C3

Headquarters, U.S. Department of the Army, *Operations Against Irregular Forces*, Field Manual 31-15, Washington, D.C., May 1961.

———, *Counterinsurgency*, Field Manual 3-24, Washington, D.C., December 2006.

———, *Operations*, Field Manual 3-0, Washington, D.C., February 2008.

———, *Army Special Operations Forces*, Field Manual 3-05, Washington, D.C., December 2010.

Hilley, Monique, "Navy, CG Training to Combat Piracy," Navy News, January 20, 2009.

HQDA—*see* Headquarters, U.S. Department of the Army.

Houreld, Katharine, "Somali Pirates, Security Personnel in 4 Shootouts," Associated Press, March 5, 2010a. As of August 24, 2011:
http://www.guardian.co.uk/world/feedarticle/8975614

———, "Warships Fill Up with Pirates After Kenya Balks," Associated Press, April 16, 2010b. As of August 24, 2011:
http://www.boston.com/news/world/africa/articles/2010/04/15/warships_fill_up_with_pirates_after_kenya_balks/

Houreld, Katharine, and Mike Corder, "Navies Ask: What Do You Do with a Captured Pirate?" Associated Press, April 18, 2009.

IISS—*see* International Institute for Strategic Studies.

IMB—*see* International Maritime Bureau.

International Institute for Strategic Studies, "Sri Lanka's Peace Process," *Strategic Comments*, Vol. 10, No. 3, April 2004.

International Maritime Bureau, *Piracy and Armed Robbery at Sea: Annual Report 2008*, London, January 2009.

———, *Piracy and Armed Robbery Against Ships: Annual Report, 1 January–31 December 2009*, London, January 2010a.

———, *Piracy and Armed Robbery Against Ships: Report for the Period 1 January–30 June 2010*, London, July 2010b.

———, *Piracy and Armed Robbery Against Ships: Report for the Period 1 January–30 September 2011*, London, October 2011.

———, *Piracy and Armed Robbery Against Ships: Report for the Period 1 January–31 December 2011*, London, January 2012.

International Maritime Organization and World Food Programme, United Nations, "Coordinated Action Urged: Piracy Threatens UN Lifeline to Somalia," October 7, 2009.

Ishani, Maryam, and Federico Manfredi, "The Evolution of Colombia's Narco-Submarines," *Huffington Post*, October 7, 2009. As of August 24, 2011: http://www.huffingtonpost.com/maryam-ishani/the-evolution-of-colombia_b_312539.html

Jayasiri, Sunil, "LTTE Boats Destroyed, Sea Tigers Killed," *Daily Mirror* (Sri Lanka), June 21, 2007a.

———, "LTTE Gets Equipment from Japan," *Daily Mirror* (Sri Lanka), June 26, 2007b.

Joint Special Operations Task Force–Philippines Public Affairs, "JSOTF-P Fact Sheet," April 1, 2009.

Joint Warfighting Center, *Irregular Warfare Special Study*, Norfolk, Va.: U.S. Joint Forces Command, August 4, 2006. As of August 24, 2011: http://merln.ndu.edu/archive/DigitalCollections/IrregWarfareSpecialStudy.pdf

JSOTF-P—*see* Joint Special Operations Task Force–Philippines.

Karniol, Robert, "Communist Threat Still a Priority," *Straits Times* (Singapore), December 15, 2008.

"Kenya Opens Fast-Track Piracy Court in Mombasa," BBC News, June 24, 2010. As of August 24, 2011: http://www.bbc.co.uk/news/10401413

King, Gary, Robert O. Keohane, and Sidney Verba, *Designing Social Inquiry: Scientific Inference in Qualitative Research*, Princeton, N.J.: Princeton University Press, 1994.

Kraul, Chris, "'Top Guns' of Tumaco Keep Coca Crops in Check," *Los Angeles Times*, December 16, 2009. As of August 24, 2011: http://articles.latimes.com/2009/dec/16/world/la-fg-coca-pilot16-2009dec16

"Lanka Suspects Submarine in Thailand to be LTTE's," *Times of India*, July 16, 2000.

"Lashkar-e-Toiba: 'Army of the Pure,'" South Asia Terrorism Portal, undated. As of August 24, 2011:
http://www.satp.org/satporgtp/countries/india/states/jandk/terrorist_outfits/lashkar_e_toiba.htm

Leinward, Donna, "U.S. Targets Pirates on Somali Coast," *USA Today*, July 21, 2008.

"LTTE Suicide Kit Assembly Plant in Dehiwala Raided," *The Island* (Sri Lanka), March 14, 2001.

MacFarquhar, Neil, "U.S. Proposes Going Ashore to Hunt Pirates," *New York Times*, December 11, 2008.

Magnier, Mark, "Sri Lanka's Next Task: Win the Peace," *Los Angeles Times*, May 20, 2009.

Maliti, Tom, "UN Donors to Give $9.3M on Piracy Cases," *Bloomberg Businessweek*, June 15, 2010.

Marcella, Gabriel, *Plan Colombia: The Strategic and Operational Imperatives*, Carlisle, Pa.: Strategic Studies Institute, U.S. Army War College, April 2001.

McDermott, Jeremy, "Generational Shift," *Jane's Intelligence Review*, February 2010.

McDonald, Mark, "Tamils Offer a Cease-Fire," *New York Times*, February 24, 2009a.

———, "Record Number of Somali Pirate Attacks in 2009," *New York Times*, December 29, 2009b.

McDonald, Mark, and Alan Cowell, "Sri Lankans Say Rebels Crushed and Leader Killed," *New York Times*, May 19, 2009.

McElroy, Damien, "Mumbai Attacks: Foreign Governments Criticize India's Response," *Daily Telegraph* (UK), November 28, 2008.

McKenna, Thomas M., *Muslim Rulers and Rebels: Everyday Politics and Armed Separatism in the Southern Philippines*, Berkeley, Calif.: University of California Press, 1998.

McQuilkin, William C., *Operation Sealords: A Front in a Frontless War, an Analysis of the Brown Water Navy in Vietnam*, thesis, Ft. Leavenworth, Kan.: U.S. Army Command and General Staff College, 1997.

Meislin, Richard J., "Sandinistas Under Siege," *New York Times*, October 17, 1983.

Miller, T. Christian, "Foreign Pilots Hired to Boost U.S. Drug War," *Los Angeles Times*, August 18, 2001.

Milmo, Cahal, "Insurance Firms Plan Private Navy to Take on Somali Pirates," *The Independent* (UK), September 28, 2010.

Mojon, Jean-Marc, "In the Heart of the Somali Pirates' Lair," Agence France Presse, September 2, 2010.

Moroney, Jennifer D. P., and Joe Hogler, with Benjamin Bahney, Kim Cragin, David R. Howell, Charlotte Lynch, and S. Rebecca Zimmerman, *Building Partner Capacity to Combat Weapons of Mass Destruction*, Santa Monica, Calif.: RAND Corporation, MG-783-DTRA, 2009. As of August 24, 2011: http://www.rand.org/pubs/monographs/MG783.html

Mullins, Mark, "U.S. Navy Irregular Warfare," briefing, Navy Irregular Warfare Office, undated.

Murphy, Martin, "Maritime Threat: Tactics and Technology of the Sea Tigers," *Jane's Intelligence Review*, June 2006.

———, *Small Boats, Weak States, Dirty Money: Piracy and Maritime Terrorism in the Modern World*, New York: Columbia University Press, 2009.

Mutual Defense Treaty Between the United States and the Republic of the Philippines, August 30, 1951. As of August 24, 2011: http://avalon.law.yale.edu/20th_century/phil001.asp

Mydans, Seth, "Roadblocks to Peace in Postwar Sri Lanka," *International Herald Tribune*, March 23, 2009.

National Security Council, *Countering Piracy off the Horn of Africa: Partnership and Action Plan*, Washington, D.C., December 2008. As of August 24, 2011: http://www.marad.dot.gov/documents/Countering_Piracy_Off_The_Horn_of_Africa_-_Partnership__Action_Plan.pdf

NATO—*see* North Atlantic Treaty Organization.

"NATO to Send New Somalia Anti-Piracy Force Within a Month," Deutsche Presse-Agentur, June 12, 2009.

Newton, Richard D., Travis Homiak, Kelly H. Smith, Isaac J. Peltier, and D. J. White, *Contemporary Security Challenges: Irregular Warfare and Indirect Approaches*, Hurlburt Field, Fla.: Joint Special Operations University, Report 09-3, February 2009.

"Nicaraguan Guerrillas Report Laying Mines at a Key Port," United Press International, October 8, 1983. As of August 24, 2011: http://www.nytimes.com/1983/10/08/world/nicaraguan-guerrillas-report-laying-mines-at-a-key-port.html

Nichiporuk, Brian, Clifford A. Grammich, Angel Rabasa, and Julie DaVanzo, *Demographics and Security in Maritime Southeast Asia*, Washington, D.C.: Edmund A. Walsh School of Foreign Service, Georgetown University, 2006. As of August 24, 2011: http://www.rand.org/pubs/reprints/RP1219.html

Niksch, Larry, *Abu Sayyaf: Target of Philippine-U.S. Anti-Terrorism Cooperation*, Washington, D.C.: Congressional Research Service, April 8, 2003.

Nincic, Donna, "Maritime Piracy in Africa: The Humanitarian Dimension," *African Security Review*, Vol. 18, No. 3, 2009, pp. 1–16.

North, Oliver L., and Constantine Menges, "Special Activities in Nicaragua," memorandum to Robert C. McFarlane, National Security Advisor, Iran Contra Committees Exhibit OLN-177, March 2, 1984.

North Atlantic Treaty Organization, "Operation Ocean Shield," web page, August 25, 2009. As of August 24, 2011:
http://www.nato.int/shape/news/2009/08/090825a.html

O'Rourke, Ronald, *Navy Irregular Warfare and Counterterrorism Operations: Background and Issues for Congress*, Washington, D.C.: Congressional Research Service, October 22, 2009.

———, *Navy Irregular Warfare and Counterterrorism Operations: Background and Issues for Congress*, Washington, D.C.: Congressional Research Service, June 10, 2010.

Otterman, Sharon, and Mark McDonald, "Hijacked Supertanker Anchors Off Somalia," *New York Times*, November 18, 2008.

Palilonis, David C., *Operation Enduring Freedom–Philippines: A Demonstration of Economy of Force*, Newport, R.I.: U.S. Naval War College, May 2009.

Paluso, Eugene F., *Operation Sealords: A Study in the Effectiveness of the Allied Naval Campaign of Interdiction*, thesis, Quantico, Va.: U.S. Marine Corps Command and Staff College, 2002.

Patty, B. A., "To Raise Them Up, Part 1: The Lesser and Greater Insurgencies of the Philippines," *Long War Journal*, October 15, 2007. As of August 24, 2011:
http://www.longwarjournal.org/archives/2007/10/to_raise_them_up_par.php

"Peace Process Bogged Down in More Questions," *Sunday Times* (Sri Lanka), May 2, 2004.

"Peace Talks: LTTE Not Likely to Respond Soon," *Sunday Times* (Sri Lanka), April 25, 2004.

Peacock, Stephen, "U.S. Elevates River-Combat Role in Colombian 'Counter Narco-Terrorist' Ops," *The Narcosphere*, March 15, 2006. As of August 24, 2011:
http://narcosphere.narconews.com/node/1219

"Philippine Hostages Head for Libya," BBC News, August 28, 2000. As of August 24, 2011:
http://news.bbc.co.uk/2/hi/asia-pacific/898190.stm

"Piracy at Sea," *New York Times*, updated February 24, 2011. As of August 24, 2011:
http://topics.nytimes.com/top/reference/timestopics/subjects/p/piracy_at_sea/index.html

"Pirates Seize Singapore Cargo Ship in the Gulf of Aden," BBC News, June 28, 2010. As of August 24, 2011:
http://www.bbc.co.uk/news/10434451

"Plan Colombia and Beyond: Guaviare (2)—The Security Situation," Washington, D.C.: Colombia Program, Center for International Policy, April 24, 2008. As of August 24, 2011:
http://www.cipcol.org/?p=588

Ponnambalam, Kumar, "The Only Solution to the Tamil National Problem," *Weekend Express* (Sri Lanka), November 7–8, 1998. Republished, as of August 24, 2011:
http://www.sangam.org/articles/view/?id=364

"President Approves Deployment to Gulf of Aden," *YLE Utiset* (Finland), September 14, 2010. As of August 24, 2011:
http://yle.fi/uutiset/news/2010/09/president_approves_deployment_to_gulf_of_aden_1980258.html

Program for Total Conflict Leadership, "Puntland and Piracy Activities," unpublished document provided to authors, July 2006.

Puello, Gabe, and Robert Smith, "LCEs in OEF-Philippines," *Desert Warrior*, Vol. 6, No. 39, October 4, 2007.

Rabasa, Angel, Robert D. Blackwill, Peter Chalk, Kim Cragin, C. Christine Fair, Brian A. Jackson, Brian Michael Jenkins, Seth G. Jones, Nathaniel Shestak, and Ashley J. Tellis, *The Lessons of Mumbai*, Santa Monica, Calif.: RAND Corporation, OP-249-RC, 2009. As of December 14, 2010:
http://www.rand.org/pubs/occasional_papers/OP249.html

Rabasa, Angel, Steven Boraz, Peter Chalk, Kim Cragin, Theodore W. Karasik, Jennifer D. P. Moroney, Kevin A. O'Brien, and John E. Peters, *Ungoverned Territories: Understanding and Reducing Terrorism Risks*, Santa Monica, Calif.: RAND Corporation, MG-561-AF, 2007. As of August 24, 2011:
http://www.rand.org/pubs/monographs/MG561.html

Rahman, B., *Maritime Terrorism: An Indian Perspective*, Nodia, India: South Asia Analysis Group, Topical Paper No. 1154, October 29, 2004.

Ramachandran, Sudha, "The Sea Tigers of Tamil Eelam," *Asia Times Online*, August 31, 2006. As of August 24, 2011:
http://www.atimes.com/atimes/South_Asia/HH31Df01.html

Reagan, Ronald, National Security Decision Directive 17, Cuba and Central America, January 4, 1982.

Richelson, Jeffrey T., *The Wizards of Langley: Inside the CIA's Directorate of Science and Technology*, Boulder, Colo.: Westview, 2002.

Rosenau, William, "Subversion and Terrorism: Understanding and Countering the Threat," in *The MIPT Terrorism Annual 2006*, Oklahoma City, Okla.: National Memorial Institute for the Prevention of Terrorism, 2006, pp. 53–69.

Rosenberg, Matthew, "AP IMPACT: An Investigation into Fundraising and Weapons Smuggling by Sri Lanka's Tamil Tigers," Associated Press, November 6, 2007.

"RSS Endurance to the Gulf," *Straits Times* (Singapore), June 19, 2010.

Sahni, Ajai, "Mumbai: The Uneducable Indian," *South Asia Intelligence Review*, Vol. 7, No. 21, 2008.

Sakhuja, Vijay, *Sea Piracy in South Asia*, Nodia, India: South Analysis Group, Topical Paper No. 1259, February 2005.

Samaranayake, Gamini, "Patterns of Political Violence and Responses of the Government in Sri Lanka, 1971–1996," *Terrorism and Political Violence*, Vol. 11, No. 1, Spring 1999, pp. 110–122.

Schiemsky, Bruno, "Piracy's Rising Tide: Somali Piracy Develops and Diversifies," *Jane's Intelligence Review*, February 2009.

Schuman, Joseph, "NATO Sends in Stealth Sub to Combat African Pirates," AOL News, June 28, 2010. As of August 24, 2011: http://www.aolnews.com/2010/06/28/nato-sends-in-stealth-sub-to-combat-african-pirates/

Senase, Charlie, "Road Network to Boost ARMM Economy," *Inquirer.net*, October 16, 2008. No longer available online.

"Seychelles to Attend Somaliland Prison Inauguration," *Somaliland Press*, March 25, 2011. As of January 23, 2012: http://somalilandpress.com/seychelles-to-attend-somaliland-prison-inauguration-21237

Smith, Chris, "Tamil Tigers Face Tough Choices in Wake of Tsunami," *Jane's Intelligence Review*, March 2005.

"Somali Pirates Obtained Over USD 135 Million Ransoms in 2011, Admiral Says" *Naval Today*, December 9, 2011. As of January 3, 2011: http://navaltoday.com/2011/12/09/somali-pirates-obtained-over-usd-135-million-ransoms-in-2011-admiral-says

Sorley, Lewis, *A Better War: The Unexamined Victories and Final Tragedy of America's Last Years in Vietnam*, New York: Mariner Books, 2007.

Stanton, Shelby, *Vietnam Order of Battle*, Millwood, N.Y.: Kraus Reprint, 1986.

Stevenson, William, Marshall Ecklund, Hun Soo Kim, and Robert Billings, "Irregular Warfare: Everything Yet Nothing," *Small Wars Journal*, December 2008. As of August 24, 2011:
http://smallwarsjournal.com/jrnl/art/irregular-warfare-everything-yet-nothing

Stone, Hannah, "RawFeed: The Evolution of the Drug Submarine," *InSight: Organized Crime in the Americas*, March 8, 2011. As of August 24, 2011:
http://www.insightcrime.org/insight-latest-news/item/653-the-evolution-of-the-drug-submarine

Straziuso, Jason, "EU: Hijacked Oil Tanker Was Outside Corridor," Associated Press, December 1, 2009. As of August 24, 2011:
http://www.newsday.com/news/nation/eu-hijacked-oil-tanker-was-outside-corridor-1.1631130

Suryanarayan, V., "Sri Lanka and India's Security," *The Hindu* (India), April 25, 2003.

Sylvan, David, and Stephen Majeski, *U.S. Foreign Policy in Perspective: Clients, Enemies and Empire*, London: Routledge, 2009. Supplementary materials and data, as of August 24, 2011:
http://www.us-foreign-policy-perspective.org/index.php?id=314

"Thailand Sends Two Warships to Tackle Somali Pirates," *The Nation* (Thailand), November 11, 2010.

Tierney, John J., *Chasing Ghosts: Unconventional Warfare in American History*, Washington, D.C.: Potomac Books, 2006.

UK House of Commons Foreign Affairs Committee, Piracy off the Coast of Somalia, London: The Stationery Office, December 2011. As of January 23, 2012:
http://www.publications.parliament.uk/pa/cm201012/cmselect/cmfaff/1318/1318.pdf

"UN Maritime Agency Welcomes Security Council Action on Somali Piracy," UN News Centre, June 3, 2008. As of August 24, 2011:
http://www.un.org/apps/news/story.asp?NewsID=26893&Cr=somalia&Cr1

UN—*see* United Nations.

United Nations, "Contact Group on Piracy off the Coast of Somalia," January 14, 2009. As of October 5, 2010:
http://www.marad.dot.gov/documents/Establishment_of_CGPCS_1-14-2009.pdf

United Nations Secretary-General, *Report of the Secretary-General on Possible Options to Further the Aim of Prosecuting and Imprisoning Persons Responsible for Acts of Piracy and Armed Robbery at Sea off the Coast of Somalia, Including, in Particular, Options for Creating Special Domestic Chambers Possibly with International Components, a Regional Tribunal or an International Tribunal and Corresponding Imprisonment Arrangements, Taking into Account the Work of the Contact Group on Piracy off the Coast of Somalia, the Existing Practice in Establishing International and Mixed Tribunals, and the Time and Resources Necessary to Achieve and Sustain Substantive Results*, New York: United Nations Security Council, S/2010/394, July 26, 2010.

Uribe, Carlos Barahona, "Colombia Bolsters Fight Against Narco-Submarines," *Inforsurhoy.com*, April 29, 2011. As of August 24, 2011: http://www.infosurhoy.com/cocoon/saii/xhtml/en_GB/features/saii/features/main/2011/04/29/feature-01

U.S. Department of Defense, *Quadrennial Defense Review Report*, Washington, D.C., February 6, 2006.

———, *Irregular Warfare (IW) Joint Operating Concept (JOC)*, version 1.0, Washington, D.C., September 11, 2007.

———, *Quadrennial Defense Review Report*, Washington, D.C., February 2010a. As of August 24, 2011: http://www.defense.gov/qdr/images/QDR_as_of_12Feb10_1000.pdf

———, *Irregular Warfare Joint Operating Concept (IW JOC)*, version 2.0, Washington, D.C., May 17, 2010b.

U.S. Department of State, Bureau of International Narcotics and Law Enforcement Affairs, *2010 International Narcotics Control Strategy Report*, March 1, 2010. As of August 24, 2011: http://www.state.gov/p/inl/rls/nrcrpt/2010/vol1/137194.htm

U.S. Department of State, Bureau of Western Hemisphere Affairs, "Civilian Contractors and U.S. Military Personnel Supporting Plan Colombia," fact sheet, May 15, 2001.

U.S. Government Accountability Office, *Plan Colombia: Drug Reduction Goals Were Not Fully Met, but Security Has Improved; U.S. Agencies Need More Detailed Plans for Reducing Assistance*, Washington, D.C., GAO-09-71, October 2008. As of August 24, 2011: http://www.gao.gov/new.items/d0971.pdf

———, *Maritime Security: Actions Needed to Assess and Update Plan and Enhance Collaboration Among Partners Involved in Countering Piracy off the Horn of Africa*, Washington D.C., GAO-10-856, September 2010. As of August 24, 2011: http://www.gao.gov/new.items/d10856.pdf

U.S. Joint Chiefs of Staff, *Doctrine for Joint Operations*, Joint Publication 3-0 (superseded), Washington, D.C., September 10, 2001.

———, *Joint Operations*, Joint Publication 3-0, Washington, D.C., incorporating Change 1, February 13, 2008.

———, *Special Operations*, Joint Publication 3-05, Washington, D.C., April 18, 2011a.

———, *Dictionary of Military and Associated Terms*, Joint Publication 1-02, as amended through July 15, 2011b. As of August 24, 2011:
http://www.dtic.mil/doctrine/dod_dictionary/

U.S. Senate Committee on Foreign Relations, *"Plan Colombia": Elements for Success*, staff trip report to the U.S. Senate Committee on Foreign Relations, December 2005.

"U.S. to Double Military in Colombia," *San Francisco Chronicle*, October 11, 2004. As of August 24, 2011:
http://www.sfgate.com/cgi-bin/article.cgi?file=/c/a/2004/10/11/MNGST974081.DTL

Vernon, Adam, "CTG 515.1 Changes Command," January 22, 2008. As of August 24, 2011:
http://www.c7f.navy.mil/news/2008/01-january/03.htm

Viscusi, Gregory, "Pirate Attacks Cut Dramatically by Navies, U.S. Admiral Says," Bloomberg, January 27, 2009. As of August 24, 2011:
http://www.bloomberg.com/apps/news?pid=newsarchive&sid=aXR8.j52hcpo&refer=uk

Wambua, Paul Musili, "Enhancing Regional Maritime Cooperation in Africa: The Planned End State," *African Security Review*, Vol. 18, No. 3, 2009, pp. 45–59.

Webb-Vidal, Andy, "Back from the Dead," *Jane's Intelligence Review*, May 2009.

Westmoreland, William C., *A Soldier Reports*, Garden City, N.Y.: Doubleday, 1976.

Wijesekera, Daya, "The Liberation Tigers of Tamil Eelam (LTTE): The Asian Mafia," *Low Intensity Conflict and Law Enforcement*, Vol. 2, No. 2, Fall 1993.

Wilson, Gregory, "Anatomy of a Successful COIN Operation: OEF-Philippines and the Indirect Approach," *Military Review*, November–December 2006, pp. 2–12.

Wilson, Thomas G., Jr., *Extending the Autonomous Region in Muslim Mindanao to the Moro Islamic Liberation Front a Catalyst for Peace*, Ft. Leavenworth, Kan.: School of Advanced Military Studies, U.S. Army Command and General Staff College, 2009. As of August 24, 2011:
http://usacac.army.mil/cac2/cgsc/sams/media/Monographs/WilsonT-21May09.pdf

Worth, Robert, "Pirates Seize Saudi Tanker off Kenya: Ship Called the Largest Ever Hijacked," *New York Times*, November 18, 2008.